The Great War Letters
of German & Austrian Jews

Translated by **Michael A. O'Neill**

With an introduction by **Michael A. O'Neill**

DANANN
BOOKS

© Michael O'Neill / Bookfix Publications

under licence to and published by Danann Publishing Limited 2014

This edition published 2018 by Danann Publishing Limited 2018

Copyright © 2012 Michael A. O'Neill

Copyright translation © 2012 Michael. A. O'Neill

Layout & Design Darren Grice at Ctrl-d

ISBN: 978-0-9930169-0-5

Contents

Foreword by Michael A. O'Neill.

"The Great War Letters of German & Austrian Jews" is a different record of the war that spared no one, no race, no family. They provide an insight into how vitally important Jewish practices and customs were to the men far from home; how comforting the strong sense of belonging to and being supported by a community was; how deeply they longed for that lost community when the guns cut down their friends and comrades beside them. Rituals gave a deep sense of racial cohesion to an ethnic grouping that was spiritually and physically under siege. The yearnings for house and home stretch like pleading hands from the writings of young men desperately hoping that the killing would soon end – but with honour and victory for Germany. As one young soldier wrote, "May our blood create a glorious empire that can guarantee peace forever."

These poignant letters lead us to an understanding of lives lived in a very different era. They are a gift to new generations, a brief personal glance at the First World War as its atrocities unfolded before the eyes of German and Austrian soldiers. Their words are absorbing, sad, inspiring. But there is humour, too. And intense poignancy when we see that they were all written at the very beginning of the Great War in 1914. How many of the young lives, whose determined voices sound out over the decades through these letters, would have heard the bells ring out all over Europe for the armistice four years later?

The unflinching patriotism of Jewish youth seems all the more heartbreaking in the light of what we know about the events that would take place just twenty short years after the Great War ended.

The desire to prove themselves the equal of their non-Jewish comrades, buoyed by centuries of cultural isolation, is always expressed with fierce passion. How different they often found the attitudes on the front line from those they had to contend with in their homeland. Yet, even in battle, prejudice followed them: "I was finally able to prove my personal courage to my battery chief", wrote one young soldier, "who once said to me that he was surprised that I, as a Jew, was such a good soldier." How proud the young men were subsequently when their comrades accepted them simply as brave men, as this quote shows: "Well, I have thoroughly destroyed the fairytale about "Jewish cowardice" in our regiment at least. And should I receive no other award then the knowledge of this is more than enough."

"The Great War Letters of German & Austrian Jews 1914" is a valuable, vital piece of historical documentation. Through the letters, trench life as it was experienced by those who were once denigrated as being the enemies of civilisation, becomes real to us. Jews were involved in warfare on all sides of the conflict; approximately 350,000 of them fought for the Russians. In the Austro-Hungarian Army there were approximately 100,000 Jews and about 40,000 fought with the German forces. An estimated 20,000 Jews fought for the British and French. In total, 12,000 Jewish soldiers were killed fighting for their German fatherland, doubtless many, perhaps all of those who wrote the war letters contained in this book. The total number of casualties for all nations involved in the First World War is estimated at 37,000,500, of which 15,000,000 were killed.

The fighting in Eastern Europe took place over an area that housed some four million Jews. In Russia, the Jewish inhabitants were initially glad to show their patriotism until accusations of collaboration with the German enemy began to circulate prompting mass deportations. Thereafter, their sympathies lay with the German and Austro-Hungarian cause against the Russians. In the UK and the USA, the Jewish population also came under suspicion for disloyalty once they had expressed their dislike of Russia, the British and Americans' ally in the fighting.

Once Russia had withdrawn from the war, Leon Trotsky, a Russian Jew (whose real name was Lev Davidovich Bronstein), became a prominent leader of the communist revolution in Russia. His actions, together with the "stab in the back" accusation – which focused blame for Germany's defeat in the Great War onto German Jews – had a powerful, negative effect on attitudes towards them in their homeland. The Jews, despite their sacrifices in the First World War trenches, equal to all who fought, found themselves vilified once more.

The penultimate letter, a very emotional one about the loss of a dear friend during a vicious battle, was written in Yiddish, in the Galician dialect. I have not only translated but also transcribed the original so that this wonderful linguistic amalgam of two cultures, German and Hebrew, is represented in the book, as it deserves to be.

This compilation of letters raises a wealth of questions; about life and dying, of course, but also about true friendship, love, learning, humane and inhumane behaviour, prejudice, and the role of religion during war and in peacetime. Answers can be found in the letters, too; despite our differences they are the same for us all.

"The Great War Letters of German & Austrian Jews 1914" is a celebration, a memorial to all Jewish soldiers.

Introduction by Eugen Tannenbaum.

The war letter is the messenger of innumerable destinies. Even if it was written weeks and months ago, it carries the stamp of experience, is somehow an expression of the great events, history in a visible form. Even if the people who wrote them are unknown to us, this does not lessen the attraction of their de scriptions. On the contrary. The narrower the circle of people to whom the writer is writing, the more moving the destiny that has been pressed into words precisely because it is an expression of personal concerns.

The spirit of the old Hebrew prayer in which the pious Jew praises God for allowing him to experience these times, speaks through all the letters united into this collection.
The deciding factor for the use of a letter was the pronounced relationship of the writer to Judaism and which school of thought he belonged to was irrelevant. So neither the clumsy lines of a small town Jew nor the writings of an intellectual were scorned. A representative of liberal Judaism was allowed to speak as was the disciple of traditional teaching. And alongside the utterances of the Zionist are written those of the German citizen of Jewish belief.

Most of the letters reprinted here have never been published before and are printed unabridged insofar as military and private considerations made this possible.

Berlin April 1915.

Chapter 1

Farewell.

The following letter was left by a cattle dealer from a small town in Bavaria, father of 7 children, who went to war on the 3rd of August 1914.

My loved ones!

If these are to be my last lines, then farewell; fear God and keep to his Torah. I commend my children to Almighty God, may he raise them to be great in Israel. I will take revenge for the many murders and tortures committed against Jews by our enemies. There are eighteen Jews here who have volunteered for the army, and I do not want to stay behind. I want to fulfill my Jewish duty! And if we do not return alive then we will find eternal life, nonetheless, with Him, the One who makes the decisions about our prosperity and adversity. We take our leave in tears, but we march out for our women and children in order to do our duty; how could I still walk upright amongst my fellow citizens or pray before God if I wanted to stay behind!

I searched my own soul and consulted my relatives, and listening to my mother's voice, who also advised our dear Emil to do the same, I went.

Should I be permitted to return to my dear ones, then I shall come back without sin, without fault. I read through the five books of Moses, I engrossed myself in the story of Abraham, Moshe, Joshua, Deborah, the Judges and the Maccabees for two nights, and I came to the conclusion that we must protect our fatherland, our family and our belief, whatever the circumstances.

A double responsibility.

Dearest father!

At the moment I am in Jaroslau, or rather, in a small place four hours away from Jaroslau. The "Deutschmeister" and 84s are in our brigade, so they are all Viennese.

We shall be advancing against the enemy in a few days. Because you are a man, I know I can write this to you without worrying so that you know for certain what's going on. I am putting my fate in God's hands. Look after dear mother and comfort and reassure her. I am not afraid, and our people are burning to receive their baptism of fire. As a Jewish officer I have a double responsibility to prove myself courageous and diligent. I think of you day and night and I shall not stop thinking of you.

May God be with me and with you all, and to you, my dear father, I send a kiss from your son, who will love you until his last breath.

Poldi.

Entertainment for the soldiers
in Galicia.

Kolmea, 29th of August.

Precious parents!

Although I have already written to you today, I am writing again to tell you about some interesting, genuinely Jewish behaviour. I was on leave this morning and I was in the town. As I was approaching Ring Square, I noticed an unusual amount of activity even for wartime. Finally, I looked into Rudolf Street, the street that the local tram drives down, and saw a huge crowd of people. I made enquiries, and was told the news that the army was going to march through Kolmea, and it would make its way through Rudolf Street. You should have seen it. The Jewish families that make up most of the population had brought out long tables with all kinds of things to eat and drink in order to refresh the soldiers marching through. There were women and children in Sunday dresses standing everywhere and they were cutting cake and slices of bread. In the meantime, the men had brought out barrels and tankards full of water. It was a strange sight; in front of one house there was a group of older Jews in silk caftans, sleeves rolled up, standing around a barrel. Some of them were hacking ice into small pieces and threw them into a barrel full of water, the others were cutting lemons into thin slices and crushing several caps of sugar. In the meantime, an old, venerable Jew with a white beard stirred the refreshing lemonade with a long spoon. One could tell that the people, all good business people, would gladly have given all that they owned in order to refresh the soldiers they were expecting. An old Jewish lady came out of an alleyway with a bowlful of roasted apples. She, too, wanted to contribute something. One table was especially busy. Young Jewish girls were standing there in their finest clothes making small parcels. In each one they put a cake, two slices of bread spread with butter (all huge amounts of war rations), two sour gherkins, several biscuits and ten cigarettes. I saw a pile of some 500 packets, and they were still packing and new supplies were being brought in. The soda water factory owners, every one of them was Jewish, had also done their part and had set up large soda-water stations.

Suddenly, one could see a long column of provisions wagons escorted by soldiers from the transport companies, coming from the direction of the station. Everyone immediately ran towards the approaching men and the officer riding at the front found it difficult to choose from amongst the various drinks of milk, wine, soda-water, lemonade and so on that were handed to him from all sides. But it was no easier for the soldiers and civilians travelling along with them. A veritable hailstorm of fruit, bread rolls, cakes, pastries and cigarettes came down on top of them. On every side there were outstretched hands holding refreshing drinks, indeed, even hay bundles were dragged up for the horses. In the meantime, we had found out that the military had also arrived by train. People hurried over to the station immediately ready to help, bringing refreshments and food. This lasted until late in the afternoon. No one thought about a midday meal at all. Uncle Schmaje had set up a refreshment stall, too. He had something very special; all the women from the nearby streets had brought him their pots of sour milk, which they had intended to use on the Sabbath afternoon, and they waited for the soldiers. Sadly, I was unable to see the reception myself as I had to return to the hospital.

Today, 1,800 Ruthenian scouts left Kolmea (Ruthenian territory is now partly in Belarus, northern Ukraine and western Russia, and small areas of northeast Slovakia and eastern Poland - ed. note); last week the Polish and Jewish scouts left. The streets are filled with volunteers walking around and singing:

Hurra chłopcy hurra ha!
Od Warszawy, do Petersburga!
Za moskalami marsz, marsz!

(Hooray, boys, hooray, ha!
From Warsaw to Petersburg
Go after the Russians, march, march!).

The baptism of fire.

The well-known writer Frau Henriette Fürth from Frankfurt on the River Main, made the following letter available. It is from her nephew Walter C. from Cologne, who is in the western theatre of war.
30/8/1914.

My dear ones!

I received your sweet little parcel four days ago and your card, dear aunt, today.

Well, Siegmund has been wounded, only slightly thank God. I had a baptism of fire for 48 hours yesterday, and the day before, we charged and shot everything to pieces that got in our way. But working with the bayonet is hard; I still have to steel myself for that because I find it difficult; but either him or me, therefore him. Brrr.

Later, volunteers step forward! Into the village whether the French have been cleared out of it or not. My lieutenant and six men, plus three Jews as volunteers. I never leave my lieutenant's side, a fine chap, so I go too. Everyone seems to have left the village. Suddenly, a salvo in the middle of the marketplace. We throw ourselves onto the earth, two men fall down dead, the rest of us get into a house. From a window I shot three soldiers, two in the yard and three others threw their weapons away. "Nitschewo" is with me. Stop, hands up! And then Wehrmann C. brought the first prisoners to the regiment. The colonel shook hands with me. Then I collapsed and slept for 14 hours in one go on an open country road. I am very healthy and now en avant à Paris. Do you want something from the Rue de la Paix? The list of our losses will soon be appearing. I am not on it. Pas encore. I will write a letter home.

Best wishes,
Your Walter.

An oath to the flag.

**A letter from volunteer Werner H. in the 104th Regiment.
Army hospital Waulsart (Belgium).**

I have only found the courage today, after six days, to tell you about the terrible events that have affected us all. Our dear, good Walter has fallen for the fatherland. I think that you have already received this news because I wrote it to uncle Siegfried three days ago and you have probably also been informed by the company. The only comfort is that he remains on the battlefield and carried out his soldier's profession loyally until the last second. We both thought that we would not see our country again. That has proved to be true in his case!

Let me tell you about the course of the fighting. Towards evening on Sunday, the 23rd of August, our battalion was given the task of storming the village to the north of the village of Lenne. The fighting had already been raging during the day around Dinant. We had been taken across the river Maas during the morning and lay in reserve until dusk. Towards eight in the evening, we received the order to advance. Under appalling artillery fire, my company advanced against the village, which was already completely in flames (because our artillery had carried out a good preparatory bombardment) and which was silhouetted blood red against the horizon. Whilst we were under cover in bushes for a few minutes, Walter and I knelt by chance beside the flag. We both had the same thought. We took hold of the flag cloth with one hand, grabbed each other's hands and silently swore another oath of loyalty to the flag and to ourselves. And then we were advancing again. We worked our way forwards in leaps and bounds. The rifle bullets whistled around us, and the shrapnel shells hurtled through the air and burst. We remained side by side, continuously encouraging one another, always thinking about each other so that we wouldn't lose one another in the confusion of the charge. The 181st, 139th, 106th, and the 107th were charging with us. We got closer and closer to the enemy, but we couldn't shoot because our own troops were in front of us and it was difficult to differentiate between friend and enemy in the darkness. When we reached the village, the enemy was already retreating and began a thrust from the flank. The command was given: swing round to the right, march! We had just got ourselves completely under cover and now we were to move into the heaviest rain of bullets. Some of us had to think about that first. Once we saw our officers, however, both of us jumped up and ran forwards. And we stormed forwards for 5 minutes with fixed bayonets; I heard Walter call me once more, and as I answered, a bullet struck me under the right arm. It was only a graze, but as I was thinking about it, a second bullet struck my left thigh and sent me to the ground.

The next afternoon, the company sent me dear Walter's wallet and diary, with the news that my dear brother had just been buried. He had wanted to search for me after the battle and that is when the lethal lead struck him!

Well, death has taken my best comrade from me and a much-loved brother from us all. We were happy to go and fight and had reckoned with everything, except that fate would part us. Be comforted, you dear ones, we belong to the fatherland. The shot struck me on the upper thigh so that I suffered a bad break, but I am on the way back to health. I cannot write any more now, soon you will hear more. Farewell, my dear brothers and sisters, and comfort our dear mother.

The life of a recruit.

I am using this Sunday, not a holiday sadly, to finally catch up with my correspondence obligations, as we musketeers don't feel like writing long letters in the few free minutes we have during the week.

When I look back to the very first time I was in the barracks, I first of all have to emphasise how pleasant it was to find a considerable number of fellow believers in our small garrison, not only amongst the recruits but also amongst the officers. This made it somewhat easier to get used to the new circumstances. However, there was also a dark side, which first made an appearance when several of us new recruits (in military language; mutton) approached the appropriate office with a request to be allowed to use ritual food. The objection was that the many other Jewish soldiers were happy to eat army food without any special wishes. And if one takes these dear military and religious companions to task about this, then one always hears the same reason: "We shall have to eat what we can get on the battlefield, and it is advisable in the interests of our fighting ability to get used to food that is forbidden, now." But enough of that.

As far as kashrut is concerned, one of my comrades has been able to find someone who is completely reliable from amongst the Jewish families here, a national from one of the countries that are our allies. It has to be said that the housewife's culinary arts, which are absolutely conform with Jewish-German tastes, and her motherly concern for our welfare whilst caring for her parents and siblings, contribute much to raising and maintaining our desire for military service and our ability to carry it out.

However, now a few details about life in service. Up very early in the morning (and even those who might have decided to go to shul every Rosh Chodesh, learn that very quickly). Then out we go into the young morning and happy melodies ring out from the soldiers' throats, which have been lubricated with black coffee. These melodies contain some new lines such as:

"... And should I die today,

Then I am dead tomorrow."

As it is enough to think about these truths just once, I mostly use the time during these morning walks for oren, whereas the tefillin have to be done later at a suitable opportunity.

The first rule during drill in ranks is: No talking! If this commandment is violated, the men have to lie down x-number of times (depending on the view taken by the superior officer concerned) in the heaviest quagmire or (which is particularly effective) in puddles or water ditches; a recipe that can be heartily recommended to the gentlemen rabbis.

Now a little about the transformation that a soldier goes through. First of all, when the office jacket is exchanged for the coloured one, the well-known phrase is: "Gentlemen you are not men, you are now soldiers!", and the "civilian rabble" are looked down upon.

But that doesn't spoil the German soldier's mood; and however great the exertions were on duty, he returns to the barracks in the evening, singing spiritedly. Passersby and people in windows call and wave; but in some windows there are also troubled faces in which one can see that the war has demanded a sacrifice from them. Then I remember with pain, many dear young friends who have only recently taken leave of me with cheerful hearts; struck by the enemy's bullets, they have gone over into the world of eternal peace. Such memories give me renewed courage not to lag behind these brave comrades, and strengthen my trust in the One guiding the battles, who does not allow the outcome of battle to depend upon the overwhelming strength of an army.

In a few weeks, perhaps, we will leave our little garrison and go off to war.

Today, I am already looking forward to the tin cans from the Free Association welfare organisation, which will give me piles of cake or apple pie on the Sabbath.

I hope that I will have an opportunity to speak to you and your dear little ones before that. In the meantime, I send best wishes to you and to all my dear friends, especially the Aguda Youth.

From your,
Baal Milchomo N.

The priest as a traitor.

An extract from a sergeant's letter.
02/09/1914

My dear ones!

This is so that you get a sign of life from me. I can give you the happy news that I returned from Russia in good health the day before yesterday. I was in Russia for three weeks, and after having had minor clashes each day, we were betrayed on the 27th of August by a priest near Wl, on the stretch of road from A. to W. The fellow suddenly ordered the church bells to be rung, and before long Cossacks, infantry, and machine guns were coming at us. We were just a small troop of 120 men because we were on patrol, and now we were faced with a massively superior force. We thought that none of us would return or that we would be taken prisoner. We were led by a warrant officer, and I was second in seniority.

We opened up with murderous fire, and the Cossacks fell from their horses like flies. When there were only a few men left amongst the Cossacks, the rest took to their heels. The warrant officer fell, hit by two infantry bullets, and I took over command.

Even though we were all only Landwehr men, my lads fired so that it was a joy to watch. As I couldn't make any attacks with the few men I had, we fired off all our ammunition, so I was happy to see that the enemy fled from the battleground at least. I refrained from pursuing them, as there were too few of us. Unfortunately, after the battle, I discovered that besides the warrant officer, another 27 men had fallen. We took the time to bury the poor men together and set up a wooden cross with an inscription in chalk. My company had already reported us lost, and when I arrived back at 11 o'clock at night, I was welcomed in A. with cheers. I had to make a report immediately. The Russians had left at least 100 dead men behind them. I had also used up all my ammunition except one bullet, but if I had thought that I was going to be taken prisoner, I would have shot myself immediately. If I get through the campaign, then this bullet will remain in my possession forever as a meme nto. I kept it in perfect condition. I captured the priest. I didn't want to shoot him as the bullets were too precious. He was executed here today. We were relieved the day before yesterday, which I was very sad about, as I would have liked to stay there. The inhabitants are almost exclusively Poles and Jews. I had to post up announcements in Polish and Hebrew stating that they were now German subjects. I hope that we won't stay here for too long. Although I went through great struggles and deprivation, I feel fit and healthy. If I feel a little homesickness, then I take comfort from my comrades, who feel the same.

A determined platoon leader.

3rd September 1914.

It is impossible for me to describe what a person goes through in war and is able to go through. Having been barracked in A., we were sent by special train to K. There, we were detrained and given quarters. The next day, we walked across the Rhine to Alsace and for the next eight days we camped on the road or in barns without coming into contact with the enemy. We went towards the French border. We took up temporary quarters in St., a German town and yet truly French.

At midday on Saturday, the meal was made in the open whilst I had to wait with the battalion for orders. Then, suddenly, the word went round: all companies have to start out immediately! I hurried back to my company, which was already marching off. I missed the meal today, as so often happens, or it is abandoned altogether.

Then we went into the Vosges Mountains, marching up and down, where the French had taken up fortified positions. It is impossible to attack these positions, which have been created by nature and extended by the French. That would mean the destruction of entire regiments. As we were marching through, we came under very heavy shellfire. Whilst we were looking for cover, as far as this was possible, we suddenly heard the sound of machine-gun fire; we were attacked unexpectedly, and the ... Company was put into the front line. We had to jump and crawl forwards under this rainstorm of bullets for about 500 meters without any cover, until we finally got to where we could start to shoot. But what a position our platoon had! Whereas the enemy was under cover in a lovely entrenchment, we were unable to find cover and were at the mercy of his bullets. I cannot describe to you what that means – to be exposed to that heavy firing for three whole hours; from one side, lethally accurate shells, and from the other, machine gun and infantry fire. We were without any artillery or cover. You hear nothing but the bullets singing and whistling around your ears, prepared every second: now it's going to hit you, now it's your turn – will it be possible to escape? Almost impossible, we all felt it and said so, we couldn't possibly escape from this position, and in our minds we had already taken our leave of the world. We didn't have much time to do it. A cry – and then another – the men left and right of me had been hit, one in the upper side of the chest and the other in the stomach. The groaning and cries for help were terrible. One man on the flank screamed continuously for an hour, but it was impossible to get help to him in the colossal hail of bullets. Nonetheless, I and one of my comrades tried to bring in the injured man, but that could have cost us our lives very quickly. Later, the injured man was able to crawl back a short way by himself and then he died. I remained very calm throughout without getting worked up. Even when the rain of bullets was at its worst, I was able to talk to my neighbour and discuss the remote chance of being rescued.

We did have one advantage; the French were firing too high. Suddenly, a shell hit the ground two meters away from me: now I'm gone, I thought – no chance of rescue – but it didn't explode. Safe for another minute, this time. More salvos from the enemy. The bullets almost graze your ears, head, arms; I hear nothing but their whistling – I have been spared until now. Another shell. Two men are ripped up by the shrapnel, one dies immediately, the other is wounded. Two hours pass, and the intensity is exactly as it was before. Then a message arrives: "The enemy is advancing!" – we are lost; a lieutenant injured, four NCOs dead or wounded. As the platoon was without leadership, I took over command. Finally, after three hours of fighting, we were able to force the enemy to withdraw – this time we were safe. No one had reckoned with that in our appalling situation.

It got dark, became foggy, and the rain came down in buckets. We stood on the battlefield in those conditions. If the enemy comes again, then God have mercy on our souls. We made barricades to protect ourselves. Finally, after another hour, we were told: the … Company is going to be withdrawn from the fighting because the losses are too high.

Then we started to march through the night until the next day at 12 midday. Through my actions I have shown that there are also Jews who are not afraid.

A meeting.

A letter from Reserve NCO Eugen Seelig, Mannheim.

My dear doctor!

I want to tell you of an experience I had: I see two young soldiers, irrefutably Jewish, who are watching me as I am watching them. I walk up to them; the clink of spurs, heels clicked together; they are artillerymen, volunteers from the Fulda region, both the only sons of a Jewish farmer. They have just arrived at the front from a garrison and overwhelm me, the old campaign soldier, with a flood of partly naive questions that I try to answer as best I can. They are magnificent young men, good Jews. We become acquainted after a few minutes, and I probably tell and advise them about everything that I am able to tell young people before a battle. Then I have to go on my way; goodbyes are said, heels click, and with a loud "Shalom" and "Hedad", I shoulder my rifle and disappear around the next street corner. I think that I had quite a positive influence on the two young men, physically and mentally.

Hedad!
Your Eugen Seelig

"Volunteers step forward!

A letter from Walter C., Cologne. (See also "The baptism of fire.")
F. 11th September 1914.

Dear parents!

After we had repelled the enemy thrust in three bloody encounters, we advanced on the River Maas on forced marches, which we made during the daytime and at night. The riverbanks were occupied by large numbers of French troops. We fought core units of the French under general Pau and heavy calibre ships' guns had been brought into position. The guns roared on both sides for three days but our artillery was unable to gain a decisive victory as the French were entrenched. They had been preparing the position for months. The general command of the ... Army Corps made us march for two days until we came to the place where the Maas makes a sharp bend, almost into the enemy flank. In a cloak and dagger action, our engineers built a pontoon bridge in One-and-a-half hours. The French didn't notice anything. At daybreak we advanced along the valley. Suddenly, we were subjected to terrible artillery fire from all the hills. We couldn't disperse in the narrow basin. My company was able to move into a smaller valley where we had more protection; others followed us. From there, we stormed up the steep slopes with fixed bayonets under appalling fire and without being able to return the fire. By doing this we were able to give our artillery a breathing space, and they soon took up the fight. At about 5 o'clock in the afternoon we advanced against the village, which was heavily occupied; we took it but many men fell and amongst them was R. At the end of the village, an adjutant ran up to me wanting to give me an order; a shell ripped his horse apart and it crashed onto me. I lay underneath the animal for almost an hour until I was pulled out unconscious but without external or internal injuries. My lungs had been slightly crushed, my right hip dislocated.

Once I had recovered somewhat, I went back to the fighting. In the evening, we discovered that we had lost a quarter of the company. On that day, I thought that there could be nothing more terrible. It got worse. We pursued the enemy, who had been given immense support. There now began an almighty struggle that lasted for 7 days.

40,000 French, 30,000 Germans. The worst day was on the 7th of the month, the day that I received the Iron Cross. We had been subjected to the most appalling shellfire all day, completely helpless, as our artillery couldn't find the enemy artillery. In the evening at 7 o'clock, my captain received the order to send a patrol up to a mountain peak from where it would be possible to overlook the enemy position. "Eight volunteers step forward!" I jumped up, but no one else did. The captain shook my hand. I crept forwards on all fours. Luckily I got to the top, but then I was discovered and subjected to shellfire that mocks any description. A piece of shrapnel about the size of a fist smashed my helmet, a shrapnel bullet ripped my satchel, another ripped the ammunition pouch on my left side. In the meantime, I had been observing the enemy position through my telescope, as calm as a bear, and marked it on the map. I crept back to our artillery, which immediately directed its fire onto the enemy position. The French artillery went quiet after exactly seven minutes. I went back onto the heights; all the French guns had been overturned. The crews were dead. A French battalion arrived to try and save the guns. At a prearranged signal (white flares that I fired into the air), our artillery fired a salvo. More than half the battalion lay dead or wounded, the other half fled head over heels, and we saw no more French that day. The next morning, we found 300 dead and wounded there. Eighty-two had been torn to pieces by shells. I received the Iron Cross.

The following days were still very hard for us. Today, however, we have achieved our magnificent victory. There was so much that was appalling and sublime; the soul of man and of nations lay open. All in all, I have to say: we have magnificent men. But great respect is also due to the French, who were opposite us on this occasion. Our regiment alone took 1,600 prisoners. That speaks volumes! Three out of four majors have been wounded and equally as many men from the ranks. Although I was hit about fifteen times, I only have two slight injuries. May our blood create a glorious empire that can guarantee peace forever.

I kiss you.
Your Walter.

Rescued ammunition wagons.

A letter from Artillery NCO, Leo Leßmann, Hamburg.
16th of September 1914.

My dear, old people!

A few lines in great haste. We have been in a murderous battle since the 6th of the month. We are entrenched on heights on the other side of the river Aisne, which we will not let the enemy have whilst we are still alive. Allow me to write some details to you about this struggle. It is terrible. I was finally able to prove my personal courage to my battery chief, who once said to me that he was surprised that I, as a Jew, was such a good soldier. So listen to this: on the 8th of the month we had to give up our position and leave our six ammunition wagons on the field of battle because there were not enough horses. The battery was called together next day, and when the command "volunteers step forward" was given, I stepped forward, the only non-commissioned officer to do so, and offered to fetch the six wagons from enemy territory. Accompanied by the blessings of my battery, I set out at dawn with ten experienced men and two horse wagons. I notified our infantry outpost, and on my own at first, crawling on my stomach, I moved towards the wagons to assure myself that they could be moved. Then I fetched my men with an open wagon. I brought back four wagons first of all, brought them to safety and then immediately fetched the remaining two, as well as a lot of loose ammunition, gun parts and our dead comrades.

Enemy patrols shouted at me twice, and three shots were fired at us. Our regimental commander welcomed me at the farthest end of our trenches, shook my hand and said: "That was very brave of you comrade, thank you." – Well, I have thoroughly destroyed the fairytale about "Jewish cowardice" in our regiment at least. And should I receive no other award then the knowledge of this is more than enough.

Please send me lots of little parcels with chocolate, acid drops, (sour candies) sliced sausage and other food. You wouldn't believe how great our need is for such things. Just imagine: despite the stormy, rainy nights, we haven't had a tent over our heads and not even a bundle of straw under us to sleep on for twelve days. Instead, we have been bivouacked in the puddles and quagmires of the fields of stubble. I am in excellent condition despite everything; you can believe me about that! I am in good spirits and look confidently towards the future!

I kiss you.
Your Leo.

The Iron Cross awarded on New Year's Day.

A letter from Private Fritz Herz, Wiesbaden.
Near Reims, 20/9/1914.

All my loved ones!

I wrote to you only yesterday, but that's not going to stop me from telling you some happy news today. Just now, at 10.45 in the afternoon, I received the Iron Cross, together with four other men from the battalion. Today, on New Year's Day. Now you ought to know why:

On the 21st of August, we were involved in a big battle in six kilometres of woods near Bertrix in Belgium. It was terrible. Many officers fell right at the start. Towards 5 o'clock in the afternoon, after appalling losses, I became aware of an enemy battery in the middle of the forest, which was sending over heavy fire. As there were no officers or NCOs around, I gathered together about 40 to 50 men from various regiments and divided them into five groups of platoons, which I commanded. I actually succeeded in storming the enemy battery with these few men. I also took 67 prisoners. These were the first enemy guns to be taken by the company, or rather the regiment. I didn't report this event because I didn't want to boast about it. However, as I have received the Iron Cross for it, you ought to know why. I am very happy, especially as I received it on our New Year's Day. I am enclosing the Iron Cross with this letter – no, I have decided not to, I'm going to wear it. Our loving God will hold his protective hand over me so that I shall return to you my loved ones, once more. Our regimental commander, a lieutenant (as the colonel is wounded) made a very vigorous speech: my name would still have a place in the history of the regiment when we had all passed on, etc., etc.

So, now I have been able to give you some happy news; I send you my best wishes, and remain,

Your Fritz

Charitable gifts.

21st September.

My dear, dear parents!

Just as my thoughts were with you yesterday evening sending you my sincere good wishes and blessings for the New Year, so yours were surely with me. I don't know how I would have felt if an angel saviour in the form of the military chaplain Dr. Emil L. from Charlottenburg – who I know through Mr. M. – had not come and provided a Rosh Hashanah evening for a small group of us – two NCOs and one of our men, two NCOs from the Divisional Engineer Battalion. It may not have been religious but it was familial. So it all went very well. We talked cosily for an hour and a half, speaking about the war mostly, of course.

Dr. L., who had only left Berlin the previous Sunday, told us about what was going on at home. We were happy to hear that everything is alright at home, that Germany's financial and economic armaments have proved their worth just as the military ones have done. We departed happy and in good spirits and apparently did something pleasing to God, as well, or we would not have been so lighthearted. I just want to mention, too, that Dr. L. gave us gifts in the form of a box of cigars and chocolates.

I was able to give everyone a glass of good old red wine from my field flask. I had acquired a whole barrel full of it in a wine shop yesterday for my platoon. Anyway, I would like to emphasise the fact that we have a superabundance of money – completely useless – and wine, also sparkling wine ... Many, many thanks for all your post. I was especially happy to receive the post from Z. and A. I would be very, very grateful if you would take no notice of the cost, because here I undoubtedly have, relatively speaking, a lot of money left over. I have possessions ... and monthly wages ... I shall continue to try to spend, in vain. It is impossible to be overwhelmed with gifts; they are, of course, shared out amongst comrades. You, dear mother, made us all very happy with your war report. Our senior leaders and the highest commander are to be admired and honoured; they are filled with immense dedication and have so many good words for each one of us that they even lighten the lot of the men who have been seriously wounded. It would be too much to say that it was pleasurable to fight, but every last one of us feels the greatness of the cause we are fighting for; and if an imperial prince himself beats the drum for the attack, as happened at ... then our achievements are superhuman. Enjoy the holidays and light fasting! May God answer your prayers on the holiest day of celebration.

E.B.

NORD-
SJÖN
Helgoland
Flensburg
Schleswig
Husum
Kiel
Lübeck
Altona
Bremerhaven
Wilhelmshvn
Emden
Groningen
Leeuwarden
Harlingen
Assen
Norden
Aurich
Neuwerk

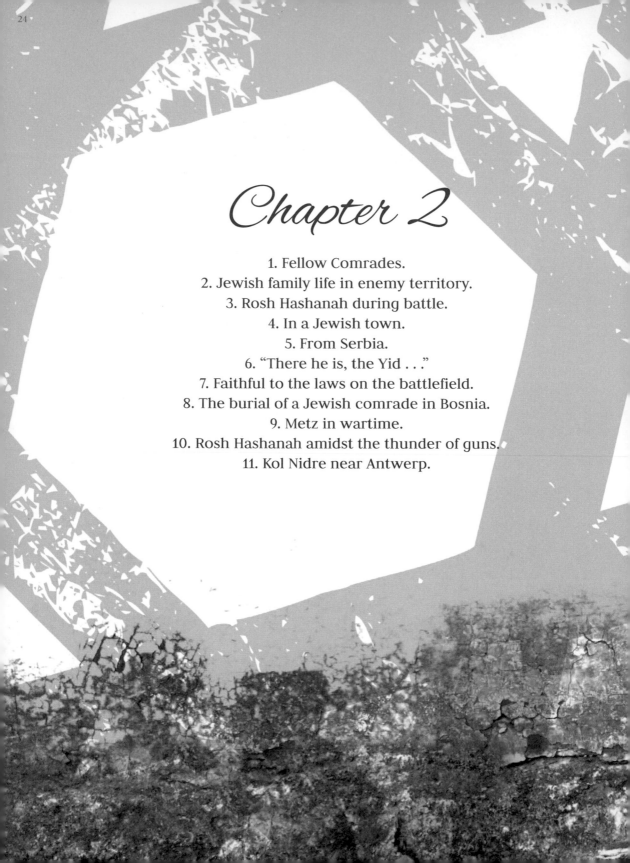

Chapter 2

Fellow Comrades.

G. 23rd of September 1914.

My dear ones!

I only got around to writing to you again today because of the holidays, which you hopefully spent pleasantly. In the meantime I have emigrated again, namely 40 km to the south of G. Of course, the town is protected by Landwehr forces and troops marching through. As luck would have it, I arrived at a place with a large contingent of troops in which, of course, there had to be Jews, on Erev Rosh Hashanah.

But things would get even better for me. In the evening at 8.30, I arrived in the dark with our luggage and some of our personnel. My comrades, who were already there, were looking in vain for decent quarters; everything was apparently already occupied. The first house that I walked into seemed to me to be the most suitable. It was one of the few houses that was still lived in and had been completely overlooked by the others. Three Landwehr men had already moved into one room, so there was one nice room available for me and two of my comrades. After greeting the Landwehr men briefly, it turned out that two of them were Jews. You can imagine how happy I was to have found fellow comrades so quickly who were also religious! We immediately got to know one another; they are both ordinary, very decent tradesmen from Schlüchtern. Of course, we had to think about forming a minyan, which could only happen next day because of the late hour.

So, on the first day of Rosh Hashanah at two in the afternoon, a Mincha was said for the first time in my quarters. There were twelve Jewish participants; a Landwehr man, a man from the ranks, a sergeant, two inspectors, two riflemen, two dragoons, etc. I was designated as the chazzan. There was one man who couldn't even read properly and who had walked six kilometres just to be here. Two Awelim were able to say Kaddish, (a prayer during a prayer service. The Kaddish is concerned with the magnification and sanctification of God's name - ed. note) and the best thing was that one of the twelve had already received the Iron Cross for outstanding achievement. Also, the corporal has been decorated twice before. An application for the Iron Cross 1st Class has already been made. We prayed again yesterday morning and afternoon, of course, insofar as it was possible with the available siddurim; there was no mahzor, sadly. Yesterday afternoon after prayers, there was coffee on tables covered in white cloths in my hostess's living room. We celebrate here, too, as well as we can.

I was also very pleased to be able to talk to soldiers who had just arrived here from the east. In this way, I was able to find out how things are with you, and I was comforted by the news that the Landwehr occupies the whole area right into Russia. Small French towns are quite different from German ones; one sees either dirt, disorder and poverty, or luxury and pomp. Our mess has been sheltered in a wonderful chateau at the end of the town. When you enter the park, you imagine that you have been transported into another world, so great is the difference between the filth on the streets and the cleanliness of the park. There is even a pond with a small boat, and there is a wonderful view from the chateau across to the variety of the surrounding mountains and the valleys and, of course, the River Aire.

I also hope that it will be possible for me to celebrate Yom Kippur in a fairly dignified manner. I hope that the fasting will do you all good, and I send heartfelt best wishes for Yom Kippur to you all and our dear relatives.

Your faithful Fritz...

Jewish family life in enemy territory.

Chateau Bathemont, 24/09/1914.

My dear parents!

I received the cigars you sent with the letter from dear father, yesterday. We have taken up strong field positions here at the border to await the decision and the army from the north. In the meantime, my duties are very boring but they are made easier by the weather that set in yesterday. I was in the Chateau Salins on the first evening of Rosh Hashanah for a meal with F. L., and I took J. with me. The people were well-disposed towards us, gave us a bed and were very nice. We sat at a Jewish table again with Kiddush, sang Shir Hama'alot, were able to do bentshing with a mezuman and were at home in spirit. On the afternoon of the first day, we went with G's comrade and another Yehudi to A. L.'s, a very bekowet family that still knows about Jewish family life. God was especially well-disposed towards us on this day. I gave blessings, and in my mind I saw all my loved ones sitting around me. And I truly understood the deep meaning of the Tefillah. I became aware that wherever Yehudim gather together and pray they immediately form a family even when one does not understand the language of the other. When they say prayers together then they answer one another and understand one another; they have suddenly become a family. On the second day I was in Marsal, about 3 km from here. The reason was that we had heard that one single Yehudi lived there with his wife, guarding the shul and two seforim and a shofar belonging to the previous community. The faithful guardian of an abandoned post.

We said to ourselves that we could make B. – that is what the old but still robust 80-year-old man is called – very happy, and at 8 o'clock in the morning we had a minyan of soldiers together, because a regiment was stationed there. J. said his prayers fervently and afterwards blew the shofar. A man named G. prayed Musaf. Mrs. B. made coffee after the synagogue as well as bread and butter. Then we were able to bless the minyan, and the good old people cried as they heard bentshing for the first time in many a long year! We were all so happy. J. had intended to keep yom tov kosher. There wasn't any kosher meat, so we agreed that each should give what he had so that we, too, could keep kosher. I gave the sausage that was sent last time, so did J., G. gave smoked meat and the others gave chocolate. I cooked, lekovid yom tov, my speciality, which I had learned how to make on the campaign: potatoes and apples. It tasted excellent and we had a dinner such as we have seldom had before. Then there was water, chocolate and simcha and menucha and tales from home. Old B. brought us vintage red wine. He had twenty bottles of it, well hidden. I repeat that I hadn't imagined that yom tov in wartime could be so lovely. There was also a reserve lieutenant with us, Dr. K. The French are not that adventurous and stay in their entrenchments, sending out patrols. The post has to go; I kiss you warmly.

Your K.

Rosh Hashanah during battle.

L,. Zaum Gedaljoh, 1914.

My dear ones!

I received your Rosh Hashanah letter today and I am using this hour of leisure to write to you in detail. When you prayed the "Unsane Tokef" on the first day of Rosh Hashanah, I and the other one thousand comrades, heard the fateful question very clearly: "Who is going to live and who is going to die?" We were in the middle of a heavy battle, and I have to thank Him for still being alive, and also the prayers that you have sent up to Him for your son at this hour. We were given the task of storming the village of C. But on the way, we encountered strong French troops opposite us on hills in the forest. They greeted as with murderous firing. There was nothing else for us to do except look for cover, and we remained breathlessly still on the ground from 10.30 in the morning until 6 o'clock in the afternoon. That was a long kaurimfallen (kneeling before God on the Day of Atonement) and more solemn than in any house of prayer in the world! Everyone lay quietly and awaited his fate, which was rumbling over towards us in lead and iron; some of the men never stood up again. At 6 o'clock – in Frankfurt (on the river) Main at this time you were probably setting up for tashlikh – we began to attack the hills, which we took at about 7.30 in a heavy rain of bullets.

Our losses were not that great, thanks be to God, because we combined bravery with great caution. You cannot imagine the solemn stillness that reigns in such an involuntary forest resting place filled with the expectation of death. The village itself was taken at midnight by another unit of troops and the French fled in panic.

Therefore, my dear ones, you must not worry too much. It is not as fiery and stormy here everyday. There are also lovely days like today when one finds calm and leisure to talk things over with one's loved ones at home. If one goes into battle once every eight or fourteen days, that isn't so bad, that's what we are in the war for, and one has the sublime knowledge that one has served the fatherland in its fight for a just cause. I have the greatest confidence that God will protect me and bring me safely through all dangers. Should God's council decide otherwise, however, then: with God for king and fatherland!

On the second day of Rosh Hashanah there were small skirmishes on the hills in the forest, which in comparison to the real fighting of yesterday seemed almost laughable to us. Today, however, we were relieved by other troops and it looks as though the French gentleman have condescended to give us some peace. I have received the little parcel from Mr. I. and was delighted with the contents. Send me some more tobacco and another two tablets of kosher chocolate. They are things which have inestimable value on the battlefield.

I send you all my love,
Your M.

A German position on the Western Front.

In a Jewish town.
From a letter sent by Kurt Levy, an NCO in the 1st Telegraph Battalion.
Olkusz, 25. 09. 1914.

During Rosh Hashanah, I was in Bendzin, a markedly Jewish town. We Jews, (four NCOs) asked for leave in the evenings and went into the temple. My only impression; very interesting! Otherwise, I was astonished at how familiar all the customs were to me. Once the synagogue service was over, we were invited to dinner by numerous people. C. and I were determined to stay together, and with our expert eyes had soon decided upon the right person. We were fed marvellously, and for the first time in a long time we had a sensible meal, prepared completely in the Polish way but good and tasty. We kept to the rituals, said the blessings and prayers. What a pleasure it was! C. can't read Hebrew and there was no fire in him! I saved the situation once more. They were very rich people with a house full of children, a countless number, a few in every corner. They wanted us to come for a midday meal next day, but we had no time. But we did go there again the next evening and ate just as well as we had done the day before (five or six courses); the people live very well here! ... In Bendazin there are 15,000 Jewish families and 3,000 Polish families. As the Jews all speak German and are mostly cleaner than the Poles, they do very well here. As trade is completely in their hands, they do excellent business. Every type of food can be found here. Otherwise it would be very unappetising here for me; now, I feel as though I have been transported to wonderland. Just imagine, there are fresh pastries and bread, there is even cake! However, in the cafe in which I ate, I did observe a boy (five or six years old) who had caught lice and was killing them dispassionately. Everyone knows about the conditions; one is nevertheless astonished, and it seems unbelievable when one sees it with one's own eyes. That is the tangible proof of what it means to be several hundred years behind, culturally. Germany, Germany above all! One gets an idea of the servitude of the Jews' life here despite the fact that trade and money are in their hands. In this town, too, almost everything is Jewish. We have to struggle with colossal difficulties as the roads are in an unbelievable condition. Deep holes, just vile. Here we met the first Austrians on Russian soil.

Apart from the parcel on Sunday, I received a long letter from you. Did you get my letters from en route? I hope that you are well.

Adieu!
Your K.

From Serbia.

A letter from Reserve Lieutenant Alfred Kraus.
"He died a hero's death in a battle in Bosnia on the 20th of October. It was my sad duty to lay him in his grave, his face towards Eretz Yisrael. At least his last wish was fulfilled." (From a report by Weißkopf, who is mentioned in the following letter.)
Serbia, 25.09.14.

Dear Robert!

I received your letter yesterday evening. I was with my servant in my dripping tent, "... for the rain it raineth every day, hey ho, the wind and the rain"; (our motto here). (This is a quote from Shakespeare's "Twelfth Night or What you Will." - ed note.)

Despite the ban, I have lit candles under a blanket; proof enough of how happy your letter made me! But I see that this war, as yet inconceivable in its dimensions and its far-reaching effects, has taught great, beautiful us, the youth of all nations, us Jews foremost of all, to grasp the sense of "activas" once more and what it is to experience life vividly.

Believe me, despite all the tribulation and the disgusting things, I have often shouted out: This is the way to live! Cum grano salis, of course, because if one lies for eight whole days in a primeval forest and has rain day and night, fog, storms, alarms, attacks etc., and on top of that a very unpoetic illness, then it is, almost, different. And really: there has been no water on my hands during the last four days except rainwater – the days when I knew eau de Cologne are very far in the past – no comb has been through my hair in the last fourteen days except one with five teeth, I haven't seen a bed for the last six to eight days and many a time not even a tent: we know what hay and straw look like from hearsay; and the filth; one can wade knee deep in this damned communication trench, which our battalion is now also guarding keenly. Unfortunately, I haven't yet been in a serious affair, as I have been condemned to reign as commander of the baggage train since we marched into Serbia; it is a responsible and arduous job, but there is no prospect of a Maria Theresia medal. (Awarded by the Austrian Empress Maria Theresa to commissioned officers who had performed meritorious and courageous acts in defeating an enemy; the highest honour for an Austrian soldier - ed. note.)

I have heard more than enough rifle and shrapnel bullets singing beside and above me, but I wasn't even bothered by that at the beginning. I still hope to cover myself with glory in the man-murdering field battles. (Apropos rum – that wouldn't be bad either!)

I have seen a lot of the country and the people on my wanderings – I was in the reserve corps at first – I behaved well despite numerous attacks: one doesn't know what is more irritating, insane heat or the continuous damned rain, both seem to be usual for this country. So, my lad, rest assured, your barracks life would be ideal for us. You and Hans Kohn and a few fellow members of the student fraternity will be saved by the soldier's life: I see a new Barkochbanerrasse flaring up! It's superb that forty-five of us have joined up! I hope to be able to free the two engineers personally. What are Hugo Bergmann, Dr. Koref, my cousin Kraus Benisch, e tutti quanti up to? I want to fight against Russia!

Organise an information office for our fellow students; get in contact with the relevant authorities in the war ministry; initiate a war memorial foundation for studies in Eretz Yisrael. Subscribe 100 crowns! Please spend 7 crowns on an olive tree in the name of the late Wolffsohn. It is truly tragic about this man: fighting first of all in the shadow of a Titan, (Theodor Herzl - ed. note) then dying in the shadow of a world war, and he was, nonetheless, a faithful servant of the light.

26. 09. 9 o'clock in the evening. It is raining ceaselessly. The last of my laundry is now rotting, as I will be soon if this goes on. Your card of the 16th arrived yesterday with the payment order for one crown enclosed. The gentleman bureaucrats ride the horse of officialdom excellently! Please spend the 1 crown as well, and the 7 crowns on one olive tree. Reserve Lieutenant Alfred Kraus sends his best wishes to all his fellow students in the student fraternity from the battlefield (and to N. Barkochba who sends his fervent love to his mother Franziska Lutzer, Hamburg) all in Barkochbahain; I urgently request some editions of "Welt", "Self Defence" and news about our Maccabee Girls Club. I hope they are occupying themselves in the right spirit, in other words, in keeping with the times; that will be of use to us for the new beginning. Has the association been kept going generally? In Sarajevo there was a Jewish National Association – glorious home! – I fed Robert Weißkopf (from the HaTikwah, Budweis, association) solemn books in Foca, all Zionists there!

Would it not be possible to make a Bezalel (Bezalel is the head artist in the tabernacle in Exodus 31:1-6. He was a highly gifted and skilled workman. The name means "In the shadow of God", i.e. "Under God's protection" - ed. note) exhibition in favour of the War Welfare Organisation? (Via Constantinople, Rumania.) What is the management doing? It's extremely difficult for them at the moment. See that you get finished with your training as recruits; in 1813 one was finished with it earlier! The Zionist girls ought to learn nursing! (I keep saying it!) The Zionists in Austria should set up a reserve hospital together with the lodges! Is it true, all that one hears about an alliance in Prague? Oh if it were true and spontaneous, it ought to shine forever! (I would get three school tests out of that)...

Yesterday evening I could only shower my head in my foliage hut, but there was an alert for the first time. Matches, cigarettes and a mouthful of rum arrived. We live better than God in France (to "live like God in France" is a German saying - ed. note), who must be living rather miserably now. Hopefully we will soon bash all our enemies, easily, one after the other. The Holy Spirit, you gentlemen of the Triple Entente, ought to whack you around the ears.

Greetings to all relatives and acquaintances – almost sounds like a farce – best wishes to all fellow students, fellow sportsmen and girls, but especially to your dear, revered mother, your brave father, and Liesel and Trudel as well, who are probably bravely plucking sharpie. Stand and go, Watch Out, (sic) and go through life in march tempo, my dear boy and war comrade! To a happy reunion, here or there.

"There he is, the Yid . . ."

26th September 1914.

The evening before the New Year celebrations, the detachment which had been selected to occupy the small Polish town of ... marched in. Two thirds of the inhabitants were Jewish and many of them had fled, fearing that we would take revenge for the appalling acts of horror committed by the hordes of Cossacks in the East Prussian towns on the nearby border. Fortunately, the small town had been spared the firing and fighting nearby and looked so peaceful when we marched in as though canons didn't exist. The reserve squadron to which I belong had been through some hard days. The battle of Tannenberg and the inevitable skirmishes with scattered units of the Cossacks that followed, and later the battles by Lyck, had imposed all of the strains of war upon us, and although it poured down in rivers from the heavens, we were heartily glad that there were peaceful days ahead for both man and horse.

Personally I was in a sombre mood. Rosh Hashanah far from house and home in enemy territory! The marketplace lay before me; the intense darkness fell quickly, and the typically Polish mud puddles in the street made by the merciless downpour of rain became deeper and wider. I was thirsty and asked for a glass of water in a house. The Jewish widow gave me what I asked for: we got into a conversation, and when she heard that I was also a Jew, she led me into a room

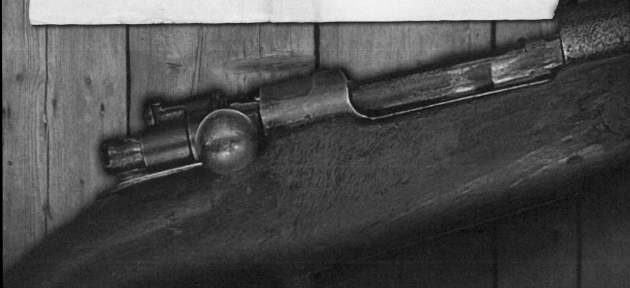

where the table was set for the Jewish celebration with two candles, apples and bread. "You must eat with us here." It was pointless to resist. I recited the Kiddush prayer, shared a tasty evening meal with the good woman and her two children, and even if the conversation, which was half in Yiddish half in German, presented a few difficulties, my emotional state soon turned into contentedness. The neighbours came, too, and I willingly gave an answer to all kinds of questions. Everyone is full of praise for the German soldiers; they are, with a few exceptions, Landwehr men from Hamburg.

I visited the religious service on both feast days; it seems strange to us western Jews. But I have never been so moved in a religious service as I was by the pleading of the men and women to the loving God on this difficult Rosh Hashanah. Countless numbers of the young husbands, the sons, sons-in-law and nephews are wearing Russian uniforms. The field post doesn't function in Russia; no one knows where their loved ones are. When the Unsane Tokef prayer was recited, big tears ran down my cheeks, too, and I don't believe that I need to be ashamed of them. After I had been seen "davening", I became a spoilt child here in ... "All Jews are brothers." The poor market woman who sells apples calls out: "There he is, the Yid, God keep him healthy", and I have to take up invitations for tea, for midday meals and dinner.

They are heavily oppressed but goodhearted people, our Polish fellow believers, and like me, many Jews will be healed of their prejudice about the Polish Jew's way of thinking. The scrounger who comes to Germany is seen as the prototype of the Polish Jew, and that is a great injustice.

M. v. d. W.

Faithful to the laws on the battlefield.

Monthoise, 28th Sept. Between Rosh Hashanah and Yom Kippur

Dear Mr. S.,

Generally it does not happen often during war that one has a few hours of free time and such a large notepad at hand. As both are available to me today, I am going to carry out what I had already intended to do and give you a short report about how I spent the days of Rosh Hashanah here on the battlefield. Also, how I set myself up as festively as possible. If one is lucky and is able to steal some time regularly, then one can live as a Yehudi to some degree, at least, even on the battlefield.

I was lucky, baruch HaShem, although keen perception is needed, too, so that I was able to put on the tefillin every day and recite all my prayers even if they had to be shortened. I am not saying that every Jewish soldier on the battlefield can do this; the infantryman or the artilleryman, who sometimes has to lie in the trenches or stand in battle for ten to fourteen days – as is happening now in the great decisive battle between Paris and Verdun – will hardly find it possible to do this. But many other Jewish soldiers belonging to the transport companies, the baggage companies, the ammunition column, the medical columns etc., could maintain their Jewishness in this respect even on the battlefield and even if their duty is often difficult and they are under great strain.

It would be very good to have kosher goods sent on from home if our field post were functioning better. I've been away from Frankfurt for eight weeks now and have only received post three times. For the first four weeks away from home I didn't receive any post whatsoever. That was what unsettled me for weeks around Rosh Hashanah here on the battlefield. I wanted to use the holy days, at least, to live kosher; sadly, I had to spend them in this state of mind and so far from all those who are dear and precious to me. No synagogue, no religious service, no shofar, no home, no family, not one fellow believer to wish me Kesiwo Wachasimo Toiwo or to whom I could wish the same and then not even any post; they were bitter days for me. For yom tov I had asked for machsorim, sausage, butter, honey, beef extract, soup and vegetable stock from home. I am certain that everything was sent to make yom tov better for me, but I didn't receive it, and I still don't have it today, the day before Erev Yom Kippur. You see, those are things that can make one despair on the battlefield, where one is subjected to enough anyway, where one yearns so much for news of wife, children, mother, brothers and sisters, friends and relatives. If I wasn't going to eat trefo during Rosh Hashanah, then I had to be extremely thrifty. I received the last post about twelve or fourteen days before yom tov. That contained, apart from good news, much that was edible. As a precaution, I packed two heavy pieces of smoked sausage of roughly half a pound in weight each, two little stock cubes and two bars of chocolate into my satchel as "indispensable ingredients" for Rosh Hashanah. My comrades "acquired" all kinds of edible things including honey and preserves from a villa belonging to a rich member of parliament. I exchanged some tobacco and cigars – which I had bought for a lot of money from the drivers arriving in their cars – for some honey and apple jelly for yom tov. I dragged these jewels around with me in my backpack for almost three weeks. On the Thursday before Rosh Hashanah, we went from Sechault to Lafontaine en Dormois, where we were bivouacked for three days on a marshy meadow even in the most horrible weather. On Erev Rosh Hashanah, we were awakened, not by the sound of the shofar for Selichot, but by a trumpet signal. Our ammunition was being picked up, so we had the prospect of getting out of this wet muck, on yom tov. I was right, I was lucky again: at 7 o'clock we marched off towards Savigny. We arrived there in streaming rain. The little town was overcrowded with the military, and so we had to camp out in the open field again. Once I had unharnessed my horses, I first of all looked in my luach to see when yom tov was. There would still be about three hours to use if we stayed here to meet the ammunition. I have never fed, watered and cleaned my horses so quickly as I did on this Erev yom tov. On the way to the drinking trough, I saw a soldier carrying apples and plums in a bucket. After a short negotiation we were in agreement: I bought the bucket full of fruit from him for 50 Pfennigs and five cigars – he had collected the fruit in a neighbouring field. Now I had my yom tov fruit. I cooked most of the plums into plum jam, without sugar however, there isn't any here.

In the meantime it was 4.30. I went into the town to look for a baker for some white bread for yom tov. "Le boulanger est parti" was the answer, but I persisted. And as I had rightly assumed, German soldiers had occupied the bakery long before and were baking beautiful white bread with the baker's flour. I soon had a loaf of bread for 60 Pfennigs. One thing less to worry about. Then I went to the hairdresser, my beard had grown wild in almost seven weeks – once more, "parti". This time there was nothing I could do, so I had to limit myself to a thorough wash, change my clothes, and afterwards, I have to confess that I truly did not look suitable for yom tov. But I was in quite a festive mood so that despite a ban on leaving the bivouac, I went off to the side through the bushes at about 6:30 to set up for my Maariv prayers. I was able to do this without being noticed.

In my mind, all my loved ones passed before me; I wished each one Kesiwo Wachasimo Toiwo and a good yom tov, blessed my dear children in my thoughts and returned to the wagons in a festive mood. There, I was received with the news that I had been ordered on night watch at the stables. An extra yom tov pleasure I thought, but in exchange for a few cigars and tobacco, I soon agreed with a comrade that I would only keep watch from 8 until 11 o'clock. I quickly cooked myself some water, prepared a tasty soup with a stock cube, said Kiddush Hamotzi (a blessing over bread; "Blessed are You, O Lord our God, Ruler of the universe, who brings forth bread from the earth.") and took out apples and honey and ate my yom tov meal; it consisted of soup, sausage, bread and stewed plums, although my yom tov mood was seasoned with homesickness. I was alone, guarding the stables: the weather had cleared up, the sky was sown with stars, and in the solitude I had another two hours to occupy my thoughts with all my dear relatives, my dear friends. These moments that I spent in my mind at home and with my family were the most festive of this year's Rosh Hashanah for me.

I didn't wait for the wake-up call on Rosh Hashanah but got up early so that I could pray in peace before drinking coffee, ready to have to break off at any moment. But luck was on my side once more; we could only get the new ammunition in the afternoon, and later, after duty in the stables and cleaning up, I had enough leisure time for my Musaf prayer. At 2 o'clock in the afternoon, I had just prepared my midday meal and was just able to say the Tefilat Mincha before we moved on to Vouziers, five kilometers away, a small town, where there were two or three Jewish families. They had fled from the war, however. On a walk through the town, I entered the house of a Jewish butcher, Scheuer-Cain, which had been pointed out to me and which had been completely plundered. Lying on top of everything, I found two tefillin that I took as mementos. I will send them back to the man when I, baruch HaShem, return from the war.

In Vouziers, our horses were in a barn but we cooked in the open, and as night fell I was able to recite my Maariv prayer. On this night I slept in a hay loft above my horses – also a bit of yom tov because under the wagon or in the little camp tent in the open, it's very damp and very cold. (I want to mention by the way, that in our column we haven't slept in a bed for seven weeks.) Next morning, I had just finished Shacharit, when we moved out with the ammunition at 9 o'clock. I was, however, able to pray Musaf without being disturbed whilst the empty wagons were being loaded, and later in Sechault when the horses were being taken care of, I was easily able to recite Mincha. There was, however, no longer time for me to eat. I had just spread honey on my bread and taken out some fruit when the call came; "Column mount, march", and we moved on to Lafontaine. We arrived there shortly after 5 o'clock. In the meantime, our gunners, who didn't have to look after horses, made a fire and cooked food. I put my pot of water on to cook again, dissolved the large stock cube into it (this time excellent green pea) and ate my meal contentedly; rather late, however, it was almost 6 o'clock. But on the first day's menu there were potatoes, with tea afterwards, both of which my comrades had prepared for their meal. I should mention, also, that on the first day by a little stream in Vouziers, I did Tashlikh in the afternoon. I found the Mi chamocha in the Rodelheim tefillin that I took from the Jewish butcher.

Another unpleasant surprise was bestowed upon our column on the second day of yom tov. An enemy plane flew over us during the meal between 6 and 7 o'clock and dropped two bombs. One exploded in an adjacent column, the other one close by, some 40 metres away from the camp. Because of the wet, soft ground, the bomb bored a deep hole into the earth and exploded with a terrible bang, but most of the shrapnel got stuck in the mud and didn't hurt anyone. When the first scare was over, I said the Birkhat Ha-Gomeyl. That's how I celebrated Rosh Hashanah. I only have one remaining wish; that on the coming Yom Kippur, HaShem Yisborach will give me the same mazel as on Rosh Hashanah and that apart from the strength to fast he will also give me the time to recite all the Tefillahs and the Vidui with devotion.

The burial of a Jewish comrade in Bosnia.

Erev Rosh Hashanah was a sad day for us. A brave, pious comrade left us, and the commander gave us permission to bury him according to Jewish rites. It was payday: for our few crowns we bought a few boards, linen, socks and the usual burial garments that are required, constructed a rough coffin from boards and set out, there were eight of us, to bring the sad weight of our burden to the next Jewish Beis HaChaim. We read in a letter from his mother made damp with tears that our poor comrade was called Joseph Ben Elieser. Accompanied by a Catholic army priest and all the officers, we put him quietly, without a funeral speech, which wasn't possible that day, into the foreign, cold earth.

After the Lewaja, we were reminded of the approaching yom tov. Infantryman Solomon and Corporal Schnabel requisitioned a prayer house, and on Yom Kippur we already had 37 Jewish comrades to celebrate with us. The prayer leader was Reserve NCO Kupfer. Neither did we forget the poor. We gave our wages to poor families who had been affected by the war. The Jewish army baker made two wonderful yomtovberches from flour and raisins, after he had respectfully taken off challah offerings. Our canteen chef, Mandel, a good Jew, gave us warm refreshments, and we could let our neworech Elaukenu rise up to the heavens at night in high spirits, far from home on Yom Kippur.

Our hearts were filled to overflowing with wistful joy. They had soaked themselves full of the day's moving events like sponges, and many, many, tears streamed down unintentionally and without awareness, over the cheeks of my Jewish comrades.

Metz in wartime.

From a letter written by the army rabbi Dr. Baerwald-München.

I could never have imagined that my initial work in this campaign would have more similarity with that of a detective than with the work of an army chaplain. There are so many difficulties in trying to find the troop units that one has to reach. It reminds of the job of Sisyphus: because once one has finally discovered the place one is looking for, after endlessly asking questions, when one gets there the nest is empty. The job starts all over again under the veil of secrecy which cloaks all troop movements; and the snail's pace at which the local and especially the military convoys travel, the amount of time lost is quite considerable.

That is why, on the evening before the Rosh Hashanah celebrations, I first of all arrived in Metz instead of celebrating Rosh Hashanah with our brave Bavarian troops. It was quite interesting to get to know this town, especially in wartime; its character as a fortress and the closeness to the border did make one more aware of the war than elsewhere in the Reich. The inhabitants had to put up with many restrictions, on telephone calls and travel, for example. For that reason, it is particularly good to see how the inhabitants of this town, in which the majority of public announcements appear in German and French, not only put up with the restrictions and unpleasantness of countless soldiers billeted upon them but also donate welfare unsparingly to the soldiers marching through. So our Bavarian troops have apparently been overwhelmed with food, tobacco and clothing. And Metz has proved itself to be a good German town even though one hears many a French word on the streets and sees many French company nameplates. I was not completely reconciled to having to remain inactive during the celebrations, even though

I saw evidence in the communities of similar acts of patriotism and welfare towards our soldiers; that compensated me a little, as did my colleague Chone from Konstanz. He, too, had been held back by a similar misfortune on the search for his army corps from Baden.

The religious service presented an unusual sight. If anyone had been able to forget the seriousness of the times because of the solemnity of the celebration, the large number of soldiers reminded them of the great, bloody struggle outside. At least 200 soldiers from all branches of the services had gathered for prayers; from the youngest recruit to the bearded Landwehr man, some in new uniforms, some injured, some in whom one saw the strain of long marches and the trenches. It was truly heartening and elevating to see that at the end of the service, every soldier, every single one, received an invitation to a meal. Some members of the community did not miss the chance to invite a large number of soldiers so that there was not one soldier who had not been offered the chance to spend the festive evening in a house.

On Friday, we were able to see more evidence of the welfare that the Metz U.O.B.B.-Lodge (Lorraine Lodge) provides to its garrison, even in peacetime. In the afternoon, colleague Chone was invited by the Chief Rabbi, Dr. Netter, with the consent of the community representatives, to climb up into the pulpit. As an army rabbi, he directed his inspiring words mainly to the many soldiers, who had gathered again. In the afternoon, an invitation from the Lorraine Lodge brought the soldiers together once more for coffee and cake at the soldiers' leisure house. This house for soldiers was founded about three years ago by the lodge and offers the soldiers a pleasant place to stay every Sunday. Apart from the lovely lodge hall, which is accessible directly from the street, there are two other large rooms in which the soldiers can read and play games and where refreshments are handed out. Also, there is an office and a billiard table at their disposal. The soldiers had been invited here, and more than 200 of them were able to have some rest from their exertions. As most of our friendly hosts had appeared with their wives, everyone was soon chatting cosily, and many of the old and young soldiers were able to tell of the experiences they'd had over the last few weeks.

Before they left, however, we came together once more in a celebration in the lodge temple, and the presiding masters of the lodge and the soldiers' home, welcomed the soldiers. I had received an invitation to address the men, and if this turned out to be more solemn than the cosiness of the hour demanded, it was because we can neither think nor express thoughts that are not to do with the great event that we are witnessing.

Next morning, I followed the troops again, this time in a wagon with horses which the Bavarian army administration had put at my disposal: every corner of the wagon was filled with clothing which had been given to me by the friendly people of Metz for the brave boys out there. Then we moved into enemy territory. We passed endless ammunition and patrol columns and several lorries with injured men and went through villages filled with soldiers. Gunfire rolled in the distance, and in the evening I crossed over the border, where the French border barrier lay in the ditch. Then, my first quarters in a French village, with friendly people.

Where will I be on Yom Kippur? 44 years ago, our troops celebrated Yom Kippur near Metz. It was due to the success of their bravery that we were able to celebrate Rosh Hashanah in Metz this time; we owe our thanks, however, to those people in Metz who organised this Rosh Hashanah celebration for us.

Rosh Hashanah amidst the thunder of guns.

A letter from Artillery NCO Leo Leßmann, Hamburg.
(See "Rescued ammunition wagons.")

My dear old people!

Rosh Hashanah evening was very different than I had imagined it would be; I didn't even have a tent. No candles, no peace and no one to pray with. Rain streamed down, the enemy poured murderous shellfire onto us until late into the night, the entrenchment in which my gun was standing and which also has to provide us soldiers with shelter, had filled up with water once again and didn't exactly offer festive accommodation. In brief, all in all, it wasn't the right milieu for a yom tov evening. I had the orderly bring my Tefillah up into my firing position; it's usually in my satchel on the saddle. Then, after sundown, between cannon fire and the lashing rain, I recited the prescribed prayers alone, sitting on a stone. You can believe me that I prayed just as devotedly as father does at home.

I have just finished my truly "festive yom tov" meal: a beaker of well water with a slice of ancient army bread and a raw onion. The thing tasted immaculate and will have to last me until this evening. I wanted to cook us all a lovely soup tonight, for a change, with tinned peas and potatoes: at the moment, however, we don't know where to find dry wood and matches. Anyway, I allowed myself, lekovid yom tov, an irresponsible luxury today; I washed myself today for the first time since the 6th of the month, a proper wash in pure, clear water! It was such a relief, and it offset the three-quarters of an hour march to the water source. I'm still in excellent health, and if an enemy bullet doesn't lose its way and find me, I will, with God's help, hopefully be with you again in the not too distant future.

I kiss you,
Leo.

Kol Nidre near Antwerp.

1st October 1914.

I was very pleased that you got my postcards on Rosh Hashanah and that they banished your worries. I didn't write to you on Yom Kippur. I wasn't able to keep to the rituals much during the day. We were lying in the trenches for Kol Nidre. There were reliable reports that Fort Wavre, which had been under fire all day long, was going to be attacked during the night. My friend B. was in a very solemn mood because he has a bride back home. I thought about you a lot, my dear ones. On the morning of Yom Kippur we advanced again and began to dig trenches. As everything stayed quiet around us, I found the opportunity to take myself off to a small abandoned farm behind the lines for a short while. There, I prayed on the ground floor, completely undisturbed until a field battery set up about 200 metres behind the house and made a hellish noise. We had taken all the doors out of the house for our bunkers long ago. Therefore, my prayer house soon filled up with guests: three dogs, a calf, two goats, several hens and a pig with piglets. When I threw the frightened animals out, they looked at me so pleadingly, as though I could help them out of the witch's cauldron. I barricaded the doorway as well as I could. They stayed behind the barricade until I had finished my prayers and went back to the trenches.

Chapter 3

From the church to the trench
– Hé camarade, voilà; boom boom.

W. 1.10.14.

My dear ones!

.... Yesterday was Yom Kippur. At 7 o'clock in the morning I was told that in... some 4 kilometres away from here, there was going to be a Jewish religious service. Our company commander gave us leave, of course, (there are three Jews in the company). Unfortunately, the news that a religious service was going to take place had not been announced properly, so only about 60 to 70 Jews appeared. There are at least three to four times that number of Jews in the two divisions stationed here. The service took place in the Catholic church. What a remarkable picture. A Jewish religious service in a Catholic church which also serves as sleeping quarters for soldiers and as the reception area for wounded soldiers. Rabbi Dr. Wilde from Magdeburg led the worship. One of our people led the prayers. The prayer books were distributed by the rabbi, but he didn't need to give out many because almost all of our Jews had brought their tefillah with them. The rabbi spoke but only a few words before he faltered and couldn't go on; he was crying.

Now, at the same time at home and wherever Jews live all over the world, prayers for the dead are being recited. What is happening in the synagogues back home? No, one mustn't think of that, one mustn't. One must remain strong. The thunder of guns penetrates through to us and reminds us to be courageous. Then we clench our teeth, and it almost seems as though each one of us is smiling. The rabbi starts to speak again. He's almost whispering. Quiet, subdued, his voice comes from the pulpit of the Catholic church, our synagogue. "Each one of us casts a look back towards his past life and lays his life in God's hand." If anyone hadn't done that in truly fervent awareness in previous years, he did it now. We have never had a Yom Kippur like yesterday's. We have never experienced it like that before. Then the rabbi recited the Shema Yisrael, and we were to repeat it after him. The Shema; the first word droned through the church almost like a scream, and then no one could continue. (Shema Yisrael; "Hear, O Israel"; the first words of a prayer from the Torah. For observant Jews, the Shema is the most important part of the prayer service, and it is a commandment to recite it twice daily - ed. note.)

The service has finished. Laughing sunshine welcomes us in front of the church. We are soldiers again. We, too, are laughing like the sun, chatting, telling each other tales. There are four Jews with Iron Crosses amongst us. They tell us about many Jewish comrades who also have the Iron Cross but who could not come to the service. Phew! How those shells whine. We have to go up into the trenches. The Frenchies are getting overconfident. We want to dish out a thrashing today. Auf Wiedersehen comrades. There is a religious service again at Succot.

Auf Wiedersehen!

2. 10. 14.

Yesterday, I was called away from writing because I had to transport someone to the field hospital in ... (ca. 10 kilometres from here). There I saw our Kaiser with the Crown Prince and his staff, who were visiting the injured. The immense battle goes on. We have been in one and the same place for the last seventeen days. Thanks be to God that with the exception of a few days we have not had many losses. If the outcome is favourable to us here, then I think that the war with France will soon be ended. So, now to your lovely letter of the 23rd of September, for which I thank you warmly. Remarkably, I receive the post from Berlin faster than the post from Cologne at the moment. Don't worry. It has gone well so many times already and it will continue to do so. At the beginning and especially in Belgium, it was much worse; there were the damned franctireurs, there were scattered French troops to our rear. But it always turned out well, and I haven't fired a single shot from my pistol up until today. Anyway, I am only allowed to use the thing if an injured man shoots at me. That only happens rarely. On the contrary, the wounded French are so thankful to us. I have shaken so many of our enemy's hands. Oh, you ought to hear my French. I think you would double up with laughter in the middle of a hail of bullets! An example: at 6 o'clock, we advanced (1 lieutenant, 4 wagons and 16 men) towards H., a village lying high up in the battlefield area near S.; there were injured Germans and French lying up there. Mostly in barns. It's a puzzle to me to this day how the poor lads drag themselves into the barns, and some of them have very bad injuries. "Thank God comrades!" they called to us. The French simply moved towards us and showed us their wounds, which we then bandaged. They shook our hands just as the injured Germans did. But when I spoke to one of them in French and asked him what was wrong, what regiment and so on, you should have heard what happened. All of them calling, questioning, waving. I didn't understand a single word until I got to an injured Frenchman who was crying bitterly. I understood him very well, and he must have understood me, too.

We loaded up the wagon and wanted to go down to the field hospital and then go straight back up to the heights. There was a racket outside. Shrapnel crashed into the roof. We didn't think anything of it at first. But the firing became heavier and heavier. And then we noticed that the French artillery thought that our wagons were guns. We went down at a gallop. I tried to bring a Frenchman who had a minor injury, into a barn; he had asked me to take him to his comrades. One shell after another crashed into the church so that the stones flew around my head. Now it really is time to go. Everyone else has gone. I am alone amongst the wounded. "Hé, camarade, voilà; boom boom." The Frenchman nods understandingly, and I take off, the other comrades after me. I think I set up a world record in running, because I caught up with our troop after a few minutes. The shrapnel shells followed us, because the French could see every last man of us from their wonderful position, not to mention the wagons. We arrived down below unscathed and got under cover.

Then we were told that a wagon with injured men, our last wagon, was stuck half way up; a wheel had sprung off during the speedy run down – six volunteers needed. Five of us marched back up and with enormous effort we attached the wheel to the wagon and started off back down. We had hardly gone forward 70 steps when a shell crashed down where the wagon had been standing. But we got down safely. Our names were noted down. An award? Well, not up until now. If I get back to my sweetheart in one piece and healthy that is the only award that I need.

Now another remarkable thing. The French were forced to escape. We advanced into the village of .... again and fetched the injured, none of whom had received further injuries through the shelling. But there were dead Frenchmen lying in front of the church. Men from a French outpost had hidden themselves in the church and been killed by the shelling from their own comrades. If the fellows had suspected that our only weapon was a pistol there would have been shooting everywhere. But when I think about the "Hé camarade, voilà; boom boom", then I have to laugh heartily.

Wolffsohn is dead. Another great man has left us just when we have need of him. It is a momentous time for us Zionists, too.

A Jewish service with regimental music.

From the writings of the army rabbi Dr. Chone, with the XIV Army Corps.

I was so pleased about the last service I had to arrange that I very much want to record the memory. I had learned that a brigade was going to take up its quarters in a place nearby; the Konstanz Regiment was among them, therefore, many sons from my religious community. I went to command to arrange for a service for the Jewish men on Wednesday afternoon. I was readily given consent to do so; the room was found and I was asked: how many regimental musicians are wanted? I admit that I wavered for a few moments but felt that the musical accompaniment would be able to raise our spirits.

On Wednesday afternoon at 2 o'clock we arrived at the town hall. Caring hands had been active, and two large rooms that led one into the other had been prepared. There was a desk by the Misrach wall, covered in a green cloth and decorated with a bouquet of flowers. Two rows of chairs stood in a semicircle in front of it, and in the opposite room I had set up the regimental band with the kindly music master. The introduction was a tune by the band. I recited Mincha; as Rosh Hashanah began that evening, I followed the Yehi Ratzon with the German new moon consecration prayer. Sermon. Chorus from Elijah. I was particularly emotional saying Kaddish, as I have been prevented by the war from saying Kaddish regularly in the year of my dear father's death. The powerful, atmospheric Netherlands prayer rang out as the final song.

There is a Jewish doctor with the Konstanz Regiment, bejewelled with the Iron Cross and the Order of the Zähringer Lion with Swords. He looks after his charges like a father and takes care of the Jewish soldiers in the regiment in every way. It is thanks to his care that I have a dignified room set up for the second time. It is not the only occasion that he has given me and many other participants refreshments of fine coffee and cake (from the mothers) after the service. This time he also made a photograph of the small community of worshipers.

A prisoner of the English.

The following letter from Mr. Benno Kahn was sent to his father Rabbi Kahn, who has since died.
Frith Hill camp. Frimley.

"You shall live for seven days in huts." How often have I had to think of this sentence recently, because I am living here in huts with fellow sufferers, hundreds of German prisoners of war; they are tents in fact, not huts. Most of the men here are of conscription age and have been prevented from leaving by the English government. The majority of them had originally been taken to Olympia, an immense building like a circus in which exhibitions, horse races etc., usually take place. Later, we were all transported here to a large camp of tents, separated from the outside world by barbed-wire fences.

We cannot complain about the treatment and food. And it gives me particular pleasure to tell you that the Jewish prisoners of war were given permission to celebrate Yom Kippur in accordance with the traditions of our belief. A large tent was made ready for the service, and a young rabbi, the Rev. L. Morris, came from London specially to lead the service. Altogether there were twenty-six of us Jews, and you can imagine how we all felt under the circumstances. During the Maskir Neschomaus and Unsane Tokef prayers there was not a dry eye anywhere. The London Synagogue community provided us with prayer books and tefillin, which we were allowed to keep as a memento. I can assure you, none of us will forget this Yom Kippur.

The officers on guard and all the other prisoners, treated us with great respect during the celebrations, indeed with special politeness, and I am delighted to be able to tell you that two Jewish soldiers who were made prisoners of war by the English troops in France, were given permission to come over to our camp and take part in the service. Their names are B. Seelig from Vennebeck in Minden, Westfalia and Hermann Baehr from Haaren in the district of Buren.

We had coffee, herrings and buttered bread to get our teeth into just like we do at home, and later soup, roast meat, fruit and a long-awaited cigarette.

An early Festival of Atonement.

A letter from NCO Siegfried Rothschild.

I felt very good during Yom Kippur. I thought that it was on Tuesday, and as a consequence, on Monday at 4 o'clock I ate sausage and chocolate outside in the field, and in the evening after 6 o'clock as we were coming back, I drank chocolate and ate several pieces of plum cake that I had managed to get hold of by chance. The next day we were to march off early to a place some 10 km away. But instead, we only marched off at 9 o'clock with our objective 15 to 18 km away. I was able to put these behind me even on an empty stomach, as the state of the road and the weather were favourable.

However, when we arrived there at 2 o'clock in the afternoon, a meal was made, and at 3.30, we had to march more than another 10 km. As I had fasted for so long, I didn't want to break it off prematurely for the sake of a few hours; we kept marching until 7 o'clock, and during the march, at about 6:30, I ate bread and drank some cold coffee from my canteen. Later, on guard duty in the forest, I had warm coffee, biscuits, sardines and sausage. There was one bad moment: just after 5 o'clock, we stopped for quite a long time in the middle of a vineyard: everyone around me was picking the ripe grapes with delight, and hungry and thirsty as I was – it had become hot – I would have gladly taken some, too. But I was alright without them. And then, two days later, I saw an announcement in the Tübinger Chronik newspaper that the Day of Atonement was not on Tuesday but on Wednesday! Well, I thought, the dear Lord God will not be so exact. By the way, I also had a true Succoth experience because I spent three days in the woods at ... in huts made of foliage.

Succoth on the front lines.

H. L. 7th October.

Today, on the first day of Chol HaMoed I was granted a true yom tov joy when I received the tobacco, the socks and chocolate, but especially the picture of dear J. There are already so many gifts in my backpack that I have to ask you for the time being not to send me any clothes. At the end of the celebrations yesterday evening, we were to have our extra yom tov. There might have been a terrible ending, but Baruch HaShem, it ended very well. I had been on patrol duty all night with a dozen comrades. We had to go and find out if the houses in the village at the end of the woods were occupied by the French. Armed to the teeth, we crept up through the night and fog and bushes until we slid up to the first house like ghosts. It was indeed occupied but by the Germans. The German guard was absolutely astonished and shocked when we appeared in front of him out of the dark night. Then, everyone dissolved into laughter. After that there was warm coffee, too. We had been expecting different beans.

It would have been a bitter experience, however, if we had come along this way one night earlier; as it was, we "avoided" the Iron Cross. We still got the reward, however, because today is a rest day, and I can write this letter to you.

I did get a flavour of the Succoth celebrations; because we were in the trenches on both days, we had huts made of foliage covered with fir tree branches. I doubt very much whether our revered Dayan, Mr. P. would declare a Succoth like that to be kosher, but I hope our dear Lord will spread out the "booths of freedom" over us all and that it will be granted to me to practice the holy Mitzvahs in peace and joy on home soil.

With affectionate regards, and I wish you enjoyable holidays.

Your M.

A Sabbath greeting.

L.b.M., 14th October.

I received the chocolate and the challah just in time on the evening of Simchat Torah. I had nothing left except army bread and would happily have celebrated yom tov with that. On many occasions we didn't even have that! Now it would be a real Simchat Torah. The news about the death of Sally Michel and Max Frenkel made me very sad. It's very strange; we wander across fields filled with corpses and have got used to the sight, so that it no longer bothers us. Nonetheless, the news of the death of a friend, someone well-known to us, shocks us completely.

On Shemini Atzeret, we were in the forest all day long. At night we were allowed to sleep in a barn and had fresh straw, an unaccustomed luxury for many comrades, and it went to their heads ... On Simchat Torah, however, together with a few comrades, I had the dubious pleasure of searching out and possibly killing a French patrol. We marched out of our villa at dawn, otherwise known as a cowshed, and arrived at our "hunting ground" at about 6 o'clock. Unfortunately, the French gentlemen preferred not to appear that day. We would have gladly called them to account for shooting at our baggage from their hiding place.

In the meantime, our artillery have begun their work on the hills behind us. They're making such a racket that it's difficult for me to gather my thoughts. As I haven't been granted peace, I will end this letter a little sooner. I am always with you in my thoughts. When you send a challah on Wednesday, then it is always possible that it will already be in my hands on Saturday. That is always a wonderful Sabbath greeting! I was over the moon when I found the Rosh Hashanah edition of the "Israelite" with the rest of my mail and read all the news that earlier, perhaps, would not have been of much interest to me. And now, I write my own letter and my own experiences! The artillery doesn't want to stop firing, so that will have to be enough for today!

Keep well and have a good Sabbath.

Your M.

The work of a Jewish army chaplain.

From the report by the army rabbi Dr. Baeck to the executive committee of the Jewish community, Berlin.
Noyon, 15th of October 1914.

I humbly give this report of my activities during the time from the 20th of September to the 13th of October:

On 28th September I moved from Allemant to Chauny to lead the observance for the Day of Atonement. A demarcated section of the Notre Dame church had been designated to us for this purpose by the command office. All other larger rooms in the town were occupied by field hospitals or were being used as billets, and all free ground was occupied by lorries. I twice scheduled a service with a sermon, on Tuesday the 29th of September at 4.30 in the afternoon and on Wednesday at 9 o'clock in the morning. At the request of the gathered ranks, I held another Neilah service with a sermon at 4.30.

All three services were attended by some 35 to 40 men of various ranks including doctors, from the troops stationed in Chauny. The central section of the church – away from the alter and the other sacred places – which had been put at our disposal was lit with candles and made an atmospheric space. I recited the prayers and sermons – I concluded the Musaf prayers with prayers for the dead – from the pulpit: chairs had been set up in front of it for the congregation. To my delight, there were members of our community in the small group. I had the feeling that the day affected everyone. I was especially moved, as were the others, when the words of the "Avinu Malkeinu" were said out loud and when the Kaddish was repeated by several people at the end of the prayers for the dead; also when at the end of the Neilah prayers, the sentences of the confession of belief formed the conclusion. This happened in the other services, too. I should also like to mention that before the conclusion of the service, the church curate, who could speak a little German, asked me if he could attend the service and then requested an army prayerbook as a memento.

I remained in Chauny for a week to visit the numerous field hospitals there and in the surrounding areas. Chauny and Noyon, too, where I am now, are the main assembly areas for the injured. The journeys into the surrounding areas were sometimes made easier for me because on some days a car was put at my disposal. Visiting the hospitals proved to be a substantial part of my activities. It brought the injured a little piece of home and raised their confidence. I often noticed that they felt heartened just by the fact that a chaplain had come to them as he had done to those of other faiths. On top of that, the relatives of the wounded men can be sent news of them regularly: on some days I had quite a lot of letters to write.

Unfortunately, in many cases I also had to send sad news to the relatives. At the funerals, in which the dead men are mostly buried in mass graves, I spoke at the graveside in fellowship with the Protestant or Catholic ministers, having followed the funeral possession beside them. I always informed the bereaved about this and also about the place and the time of the funeral and before that, the details of the soldier's passing.

I then set out from Chauny on a trip that had been planned long before, which was to take me to the individual divisions. In order to get closer to the troops, it proved to be necessary to go to the individual divisions and brigades, insofar as this was possible. I devoted the whole of last week to getting started on this task and spent three days at each of two divisions. There, I held two camp services in the open and wherever the Jewish soldiers found themselves alone in the troop unit, I gave them spiritual counselling. I also went to the field hospitals and dressing stations and asked about injured Jewish men there. Travelling all around the country like that caused all kinds of difficulties and exertions.

Many of the villages in which I took up quarters for the night had been almost completely destroyed through shelling, and the few houses that still had a roof and a few windows were, of course, already occupied by men who belonged to the troop units.

As the horses had to be rested, especially because of the unfavourable weather conditions, I have come to Noyon for a few days. I'm using this time to visit the five field hospitals here. I have also arranged for a service on Saturday at 4 in the afternoon. I shall make my way to the other divisions on one of the following days.

I have not been able to find out how my colleagues who have been conscripted as army chaplains are going about their business. I have only been able to make contact with one of them up until now: he followed the advice from the area high command and is now permanently in one of the main assembly areas. My experiences so far have taught me that this completely limits the area of activity. It is absolutely necessary to visit all sections of the army, despite the difficulties. This is the only way to give, if not everyone, then many of the men the personal impression and the personal certainty that a rabbi is amongst them. It is essential that the Jews know this and also that those of other faiths know it, too. This is indisputably significant for the acceptance of Judaism, and it doesn't need to be pointed out that acceptance of Jews is dependent first and foremost upon the acceptance of Judaism. It is also important for the position of the Jewish soldier that his religion stands visibly beside the others.

Of course, it is not possible for me to do all that I wish and need to do and think about doing.

The Jewish soldiers are scattered far and wide, some regiments only contain two Jewish soldiers; the … Regiment that I have been assigned to, appears to have the relatively large number of 17, and I want to visit them shortly. There are 40 to 50 Protestant ministers and almost as many Catholic ministers on duty in the area that is cared for by one Jewish chaplain, because their numbers were considerably increased a few weeks ago. With more suitable organisation, many things could have been done better. But it is to be hoped that the experiences of this war will not need to be drawn upon in another one. Many tasks can be carried out under the prevailing conditions here.

It may be that in my next report I will send news of the very favourable impression that I have gained of the Jewish soldiers.

May I also inform you that my own mental and physical condition, even on unfavourable days, has always been good.

The bond that unites.

A reply to the provincial rabbi Dr. Baumberger in Hannau, who sent his blessings on the High Holy days to the members of his district serving in the field.
S. 27th Oct. 1914.

I was so happy to receive your letter of the 26th of September for which I most cordially thank you. Unfortunately, I only received the letter the day before yesterday, too late for the Day of Atonement, therefore. I badly needed the prayer book on that day. It is remarkable. You know my religious views and know that I do not stand on ceremony. And I include the traditional "prayers" in these ceremonies, as they are mostly not prayers but observations. And yet, the further one is from home, the more closely one attaches oneself to that which connects us to home, and that just happens to be ... structure! One feels oneself closer to home when one knows that at home they are doing the same thing at the same time as we are. And so I made an effort to keep the Day of Atonement as I was used to doing at home. I fasted, and in my mind I followed the service at home at the appropriate time. True, I myself did not have a service on that day, and yet I was perhaps more devout than on many occasions in the past! We held a service here three days after the Day of Atonement, organised by a Catholic priest. I have to say, I have hardly experienced a more elevating celebration. We soldiers formed a square around the minister, who was standing in front of a shell crater in a meadow. In the background, the houses in S. that had been shot into flames looked over towards us. First of all, the priest had us sing the first verse of the chorale: Great God we praise thee! And then he gave an enthusiastic address; starting with the concept of God's mercy, he invited us to fulfill our highest duty, and finally pleaded for victory and peace for the emperor, the Reich, for princes and the people, for the country and the army. The celebrations concluded with another chorale verse.

You mentioned in your letter that those faraway are so near in thought and feeling at this time. That is so very true! I corresponded with my brother on the occasion of the New Year celebrations with a reminder of how contemporary our prayers and psalms are that were written thousands of years ago. And now I find the same thought in the second of your "religious service lectures" which gave me an hour of consecrated enjoyment. Apart from the places marked by you, perhaps I might point to Psalm 3 and Psalm 27. And is there any more wonderful and at the same time more contemporary wish than the last sentence in the Kaddish: "Oseh shalom bim'romav hu ya'aseh shalom"? (He who makes peace in His heights, may He make peace.)

Your,
Dr. E. W.
Reserve Lieutenant.

The religious backbone.

A postcard from Hugo Elkan from Essen, stretcher-bearer with the 3rd Company Brigade, 86th Reserve Battalion of the 8th Reserve Division, to Rabbi Dr. Bamberger in Schönlanke.

Bois du Four near Thiancourt in France.
In the trenches, 31. 10. 14.
Defensive position Toul-Verdun.

Dear Rabbi!

My company commander, Lieutenant Röhrig, has just given me one of your devotional booklets. Owning this gives me even greater pleasure than it might normally do as I had to take leave of my Protestant song book, and I found it surprising that our religious interests were so little represented here on the battlefield. Now, I am glad that I have been able to convince myself that the opposite is true. I want to take this opportunity to thank your reverend self cordially and personally for this welcome gift. I shall carry this little book with me as a talisman for the remainder of the war. It is, to a certain extent, a religious backbone for every Jewish soldier.

With my humble respects,
Hugo Elkan from Essen on the Ruhr,
stretcher-bearer.

The abuse of Jews in the Russian Army.

From a letter written by a Hungarian reserve sergeant.

... The way that the Russian Army treats its Polish and Jewish soldiers is outrageous. They are sent to the most dangerous areas; for example, only Polish and Jewish soldiers were used to charge the defences of the fortress at Przemysl. When they were beaten off by our troops, they were forced back onto the attack by the machine guns of their own troops. All prisoners have reported the same thing.

There is a conspicuously high number of Jews and Poles amongst the fallen Russians. They are simply led to the slaughterhouse. There are emotional scenes here. Before an attack on the fortress, individual Jewish soldiers put on the white kittel that is worn at Yom Kippur. Letters were found in their pockets in which they asked our Jewish stretcher-bearers and those who would bury them later, to say a Kaddish for them when they were found and after the burial.

The Russian officers behave in a very cowardly fashion. During an attack they are always at the rear and drive the fighting soldiers into the firing line by beating them with rubber batons.

Those of us who were not on duty spent a wonderful Rosh Hashanah, Yom Kippur, and Succoth. We set up for our service in the living room of a small farmhouse. We got our Sefer Torah from a private synagogue in neighbouring Przemysl. We had a really good prayer leader in the person of a very religious reserve sergeant. The service was held in a very intimate and devotional manner. Lots of people, men from so many branches of the armed forces took part. Infantrymen, hussars, artillerymen, Austrian reservists, Uhlans, dragoons, medics and two officers formed our devotional public. The fact that on Yom Kippur a powerful attack on a fortress took place and that one heard the terrible thundering of the guns all day long, contributed to intensifying the atmosphere of devotion.

And it appears that the dear Lord heard our prayers and helped our troops on to victory.

Filial love.

The widow Levi from Zwesten in the district of Kassel, who has six sons in the war, put the following letter at our disposal with these words: "There are two letters from my son enclosed. I ask you for the love of God to please send them back to me again because I am a very poor widow whose only riches are the letters from my sons." Russian-Poland 31st October 1914.

My dear, good little mother!

I received your two letters of the 20th and 26th of October with a thousand feelings of joy. I gather from these that all of you are very well, and I can also report the same about me, thank God. But, dear mother, judging by your letters you cannot get over the fact that you have six sons in the war. Certainly it is no small thing for a mother of 70 years to see that all of her boys, her only hope and only support, have gone to war. But dear, good mother! Don't let your heart be so oppressed at this difficult hour. Think of how often the good Lord stood beside you at the most difficult times. And will he really abandon you now, at this difficult time? No, I don't believe it. Think of the joy when we all return victorious. Oh, how many new tales we will be able to tell you. Indeed, we could write entire books. It should be a joy and honour for you that we are fighting for the fatherland. And whoever has seen as I have, what damage the enemy, the vile Russians have done to the fatherland in Eastern Prussia, he fights willingly, and even if he can see death with his own eyes, he looks towards it gladly. I received the small parcels from Selma but not the large one. I received two packets today from Klara from Wolfhagen and I receive many from my Berta. Many thanks to you, dear little Hannah, for the cigarettes.

Dear Rosa! You don't need to be worried about Moritz. Jeanette wrote to me that he is with a light ammunition column. So he will not be fighting at all. He is always many, many kilometres away from the fighting and rides on the wagon every day. Indeed, almost into the living room in the billet. And then he is in France and it is a thousand times better there than in Poland. There is an abundance of food there.

Now I shall take this chance to tell you how we are. 1. Roads! The best roads are dirtier and in worse condition than the worst forest tracks at home in Germany. We have to tie our boots on, so that they don't get stuck in the mud. 2. Food is rare and expensive. A pound of sugar costs 1 mark, a pound of coffee 3 marks, bread is a rarity. We would willingly pay the price, however, if we could get anything. The cold is not quite as bad as you might imagine. However, it's worse than in France. It's wonderful in Namur. I was there once, as well. Indeed, I was there when Namur was taken.

Let me hear something from you very soon and I send you all my love. From your Emil.

The Iron Cross First Class.

**A letter from a reserve NCO in the 48th Infantry Regiment,
Oskar Brieger from Hohensalza.**

*This is how I earned the Iron Cross Second Class: when we arrived in Hofstaade on the 25th of
August following a series of difficult marches, we were welcomed with terrible, heavy gunfire; the
entire civilian population, including the women, fired at us unceasingly. They killed many of my
comrades. My rifle butt was shot away by a franctireur so that I held just the barrel in my hand.
In order to protect myself somewhat, I looked for cover in a barn, and as I was doing so I saw a
Belgian soldier shooting our injured men. When this vermin wanted to reload his rifle, I rammed
my bayonet into his heart. I was able to bandage my wounded comrades and carry them out of the
line of fire.*

*This is how I got the Cross First Class: from the 9th to 30th of September we were fighting in
Elevyt. As heavy artillery was firing at us continuously, the dressing station was placed in the
cellar of a two-storey house on the opposite side of the street from the trenches. Even though
a red cross had been attached to the house, it was targeted by enemy shells. I brought six
badly wounded comrades over there, and their wounds were dressed by the medical officer Dr.
Laserstein from Berlin. After the second shell crashed in, the house collapsed and began to burn.
The six wounded soldiers, the staff doctor and his assistant, several musicians and inhabitants
were completely buried, thirty-two people in all. I managed to work my way out and got to a
door that I hadn't seen before. I smashed it with a stone and got through to a side cellar in which
there was a window onto the street with heavy bars in front of it. I tried with all my strength to
remove the iron bars but only succeeded in bending the middle one. I took off my clothes and
forced myself through the bars onto the street in order to get help from our trenches.*

*I had hardly got onto the street when a shell flew down and hurled me over into our
trenches, where I lay unconscious. When I came to, I asked some comrades for help, but the
enemy fire was so terrible that no one dared to leave the trenches. I made a quick decision,
got hold of an axe and ran as fast as possible back to the house to try and save whatever
could be saved. On the way, a shell exploded one metre (3.2 ft) away from me; the shrapnel
didn't bend a single one of my hairs, however. Using all of my strength, I smashed the wall to
the side cellar and was able to liberate my wounded comrades, the badly injured Dr. and all of
the inhabitants and accompany them to a safe place, without any help.*

"Being human".

A letter from corporal Martin Feist, Frankfurt on Main, in the ...
Infantry Regiment, who fell in France.
In the trenches at Andochy, 2. XI. 14., in the afternoon.

My dear ones!

... I want to continue with my news from yesterday. The night from Thursday to Friday was peaceful, against all expectations. Friday itself brought us some peace, and wearied from our exertions, we rested, tired, in our trenches. The Sabbath began and then an order came through again, quietly repeated from one trench to another: "Pack the haversacks, everything battle ready, fix bayonets." A shudder went through me when I heard another order, too, in the same way: "Tonight, attack." Silently, I lent against the parapet of the trench that leaned steeply outwards, from where we expected the enemy: the full moon that had just risen made it easier to survey the undulating territory. I said my Maariv prayer, and then my thoughts wandered back to you, my dear ones. I saw you united around the Sabbath table, tranquil but nonetheless absorbed with Simcha shel Mitzvah.

I thought of all my friends and relations, above all of him, the precious friend with the warm heart and the glowing ideals in his breast. He was absorbed more and more with the struggle towards all that was true, beautiful and good. He was not to achieve his goal. Far from home, enemy bullets struck him and put an end to this fine young life far too soon. There is nothing of him left to me except the memory of the happy and gloomy days of youth that we spent together. God's purpose is inscrutable. My thoughts moved along like this for hours. They looked inwards as I thought of the horror that my eyes have seen. You who have stayed at home, how lucky you are that you have been spared the experience of the horrors of war. If you could understand it properly, you wealthy people, you would open your hearts and hands wider, would show yourselves to be great human beings and even greater in your duties as Jews, in order to relieve the misery and distress. You would understand that it is twice as necessary in these times to donate and to give. It may be that during these years, sources of income dried up, indeed, it is probable that there were losses, but God gave you so many years of prosperity.

My thoughts continued; may this age move into our streets in Frankfurt and purify everything; may one learn to understand that up until now there have been too many questions about who was rich and who was poor. Get rid of the worship of wealth, remove these idols from our hearts and our Frankfurt will see that there is something higher which is known as "being human". May this great moment find a great race, may it cause us to educate ourselves so that after the war we can begin life with new concepts, new perceptions.

The moon disappeared behind clouds that had gathered and darkened. I followed it with my eyes as it tried to work its way again and again up through the clouds. It became quiet and dark around me. Then, heavy rifle fire started up to my right, the guns thundered, machine guns rattled ceaselessly, the French attack had begun. The morning found us and we were the victors; but it had cost many brave comrades their lives.

We spent Saturday peacefully. In the evening, I did Havdalah with cold coffee from my field canteen.

There was an old petroleum lamp and a cigar as a besamim and I sang zemirot just for myself. My trust in HaKodosh Baruch Hu accompanied me from the Sabbath into the week and He will protect and guard me, and with His help we will see each other again.

I send best wishes to you all.
Your Martin.

Jewish life in a small garrison.

A letter from Medical Officer Dr. Max Sichel from Frankfurt am Main.
Aschaffenburg, 3. 11. 14.

Dear Eugen!

I have been here three months today. When I hurried home on that Sunday, in order to comply with my draft notice, filled with the freshness of summer whilst the Lamentations of Jeremiah rang out in all the synagogues, I did not think that I would be spared the thundering guns and trenches for three months. The first weeks, during which deployment was completed in a magnificent manner, remain unforgettable. We medical officers had the task of examining the departing troops to see if they were fit for transport. We started to do this immediately during the night from the 2nd to the 3rd day of mobilisation. New troops came forward every hour; after a medical inspection and a few inspiring words from the officer on duty, they then departed. There was no need for the officer's words, because spirits were high even without alcohol playing its part; it was strictly forbidden to hand out alcohol at any of the stations. Only occasionally did one man or another seek to avoid his honourable duty because of real illness.

Life takes place here within the bounds of a small garrison. Every evening we meet in one of the few decent bars to discuss the news of the day and to wait for the last telegrams from the theatre of war. The senior man in the garrison, the battalion major, is the spokesperson, and there are a large group of officers and medical officers clustered around him. Every evening Europe is divided up here, and it is surprising that the Russians and French still keep some of it. Of course, the population of a small garrison town is very involved with the troops stationed there. This interdependence is understandable and is particularly strong during the present, storm-tossed days. It is an event for the whole town whenever the departing troops leave for the front. The Jewish troops from the battalion here make a thoroughly favourable impression; they spend part of their time in the Jewish restaurant, which has many advantages but also more than a few dark sides.

In our hospital, the only Jewish stretcher-bearer has reported for duty at the front lines. He is depressed in case his wish isn't granted. In the synagogue, the rabbi deals with the contemporary subject of war at every opportunity. Recently, he spoke more about the question of whether the current war is the one that the Holy Scripture announces will come on the evening before the messianic age. As various signs are lacking, this view, which is held by many, is repudiated. The extremely important question of whether or not one may carry a sword on the Sabbath was also answered in the negative as this weapon does not fulfill the criteria of being decorative. On one of the previous Sabbath afternoons, he said, he had heard that a Jewish soldier had terminated his trust in the dear Lord because despite ardent, fervent pleading, his comrade had not been spared

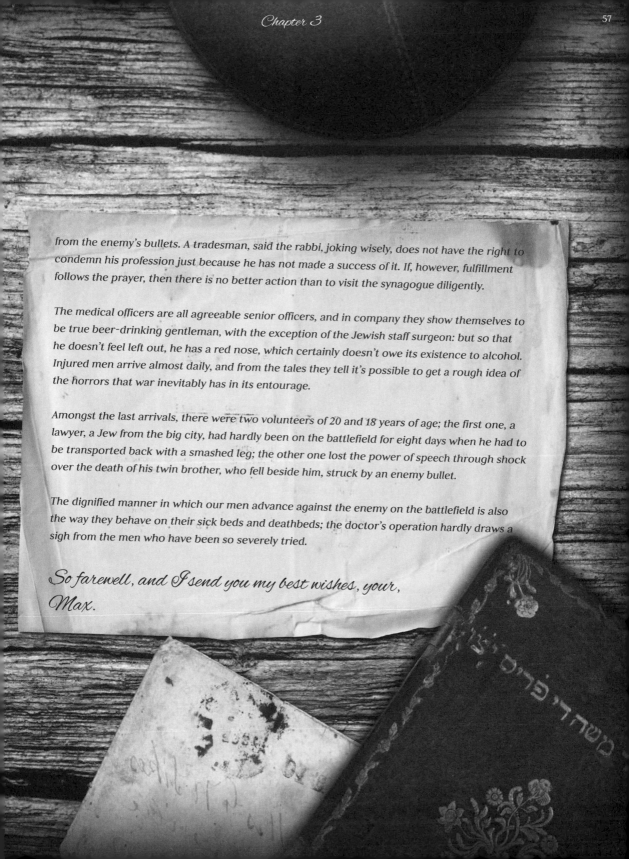

from the enemy's bullets. A tradesman, said the rabbi, joking wisely, does not have the right to condemn his profession just because he has not made a success of it. If, however, fulfillment follows the prayer, then there is no better action than to visit the synagogue diligently.

The medical officers are all agreeable senior officers, and in company they show themselves to be true beer-drinking gentleman, with the exception of the Jewish staff surgeon: but so that he doesn't feel left out, he has a red nose, which certainly doesn't owe its existence to alcohol. Injured men arrive almost daily, and from the tales they tell it's possible to get a rough idea of the horrors that war inevitably has in its entourage.

Amongst the last arrivals, there were two volunteers of 20 and 18 years of age; the first one, a lawyer, a Jew from the big city, had hardly been on the battlefield for eight days when he had to be transported back with a smashed leg; the other one lost the power of speech through shock over the death of his twin brother, who fell beside him, struck by an enemy bullet.

The dignified manner in which our men advance against the enemy on the battlefield is also the way they behave on their sick beds and deathbeds; the doctor's operation hardly draws a sigh from the men who have been so severely tried.

So farewell, and I send you my best wishes, your,
Max.

"Just a little French . . ."

B.-H., 4th November.

... It was Shabbat Chol Ha-mo'ed Sukkot. Our column arrived in G. at 4 o'clock in the afternoon, and as we were the only military in the place, apart from the small detachment from a signals battalion, our column leader, Lieutenant W. was appointed commander. We had stabled and taken care of the horses and were about to go and eat – we had set off from S. early, at 7 o'clock, so we had a mighty appetite – when we suddenly heard "Fall in!" and with fixed bayonets as though ready for battle! Our lieutenant walked in front of the column and told us that he had just received the order to arrest all the inhabitants of the village and intern them in the schoolhouse. War is war one has to say to oneself. The internment didn't go that smoothly of course. Some of the people, who were mostly poor, left their houses and possessions, crying and sobbing. Others, who couldn't see the reason for this strict measure, were unruly and initially refused to go. My Jewish comrade and I, with our little bit of French, had to use all of our powers of persuasion to make it clear to the people that it was pointless to refuse; on the other hand, we had to speak in German to our gentlemen comrades to prevent them from using force. So we had the feeling that we had done something good and that we had diverted a disaster from the people. After almost 1½ hours of work, all the houses, barns and stables in the village had been searched and all of the inhabitants interned in the schoolhouse. One room was designated as the guardroom, and I had to go on guard duty as a translator. So I had the opportunity of spending the night of Hoshana Rabbah "watching". Indeed, I didn't get to sleep that night and was barely able to "learn".

But there was no lack of humorous incidents. Those arrested had thousands of wishes and every time one of the people left the room, the guard had to report it to the guardroom so that I could ask the people what they wanted. One man wanted to feed his cows, a woman wanted to milk her cows so that she would have milk for her little children, some people needed beds, others had forgotten plates, knives, forks etc., and one of the guards always had to accompany them with a fixed bayonet. It wasn't easy for me, there were frequent misunderstandings or we simply didn't understand one another. One older woman had left her false teeth at home, and as a result she couldn't eat. It was hard work trying to figure that out. Another family had prepared roast rabbit for the evening and it was bubbling on the stove back at home. Well, rabbit in French is "lapin"; I didn't know that of course. I only knew that "le pain" meant, bread. So you can imagine what hard work it was for me to find out what the people wanted with their "lapin". It was also difficult to come to an understanding with one family whose cow, on this evening of all times, was looking forward to a happy event. A holiday of one and a half to two hours was granted for this festive act. Four people were needed to do this, and two men with fixed bayonets – I was amongst them as the translator – had to accompany them. So I had a *lot of work on the following day in G. as well, and I was glad when we advanced to V., 25 km away on the morning of Shemini Atzeret. On the way, we once more encountered long lines of emigrants who had abandoned house and home through fear of the "Prussiens" and who now had a better opinion of the enemy and wanted to return to their houses.*

France has brought unspeakable misfortune, misery and poverty down on its people through this reckless war, which these poor people wanted just a little as we did.

We have been here in B. for the last 2 days. We have stabled our horses on the large estate of an apparently very rich sugar beet farmer, Monsieur Secret, who was, unfortunately, as of course are most of the wealthy people, "parti". In a carriage shed on his farm, we found a machine for crushing and pressing apples that could hardly be more modern and practical if it were owned by a "cider- bottler" from Sachsenhausen. This monster was greeted with enormous cheers by my comrades. Within ten minutes, two large sacks full of apples had been collected, and so the crushing and pressing of the apples began. Within an hour, we had a large tub full of the "sweet stuff" that would have done honour to "A. Rackles", "The Freyeisen Brothers" or some other cider producer from Sachsenhausen. I would have to pay 15 Pfennigs for half a pint in "The Beautiful Miller's Wife" bar on Baumweg, and here I had it for free and also had the satisfaction of having worked on the delicious brew myself. Except this time when I drank the "sweet stuff", my dear friends from Frankfurt, who would otherwise be sitting with me, were not there; those friends who are not in the war themselves, recently sent me a postcard greeting from the "sweet stuff". Instead, the comrades around me here were even more on the ball, so I disappeared off to bed in good time. As you can see, the war even has its funny episodes. I could tell you a lot of other things, too, but prefer to do that later in person. I send you warmest best wishes,

Your A.

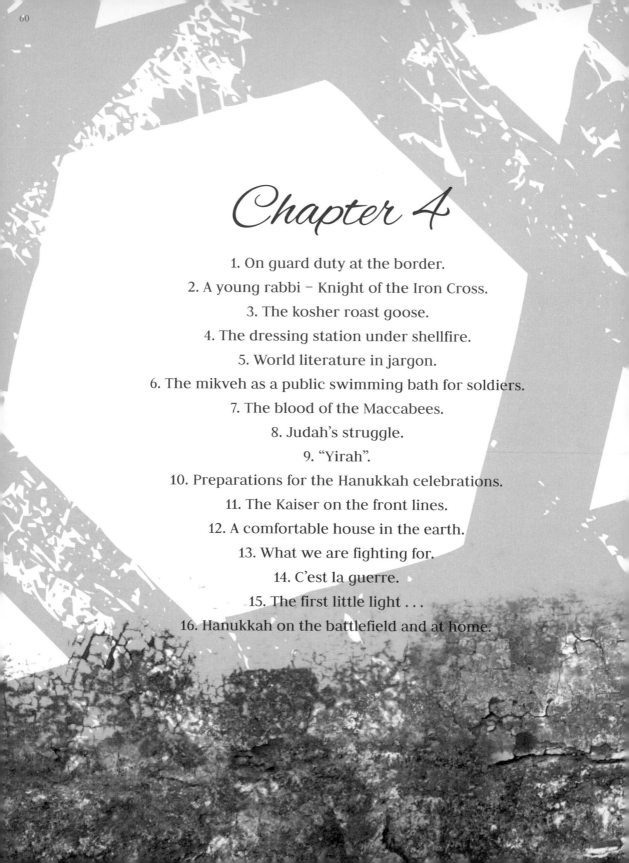

Chapter 4

On guard duty at the border.

Russia, 4. 11. 1914.

Dear Schwabauch!

Many thanks for your postcard of the 27th of October. Today I have a lot of new things to tell you. So first of all, thank you for your congratulations on my promotion to warrant officer; for the moment, however, that's a title without substance, as I am superfluous and therefore drawing a sergeant's pay. Otherwise there are several pleasant aspects that come with promotion. The best thing about it all is that I am given tasks to carry out independently. At the moment, I am carrying out guard duty very close to the border; I have 64 men and 4 NCOs under my command. One of those badly built, badly maintained streets runs along outside my window and a large number of wagons, mostly laden with grain, roll along it towards the nearby border each day. The characters on and beside the wagons, with their thick sheepskin coats and high black fur caps, always remind me that I am not on German soil.

Life has left its usual path anyway. We sleep fully clothed with our boots on, the electric lamp in front of our chests and the Browning by our sides. I quickly got used to it, and as I was given a good bed with clean linen (you'll be thinking: with those boots) from the owner of the house, I nestle (terminus technicus militaris) magnificently. The telephone beside me rings only occasionally to convey a report or an order from the company to me.

I check on the guards and the people here at least once every night. Until yesterday, there was a harsh autumn wind whistling over the countryside, and we didn't leave the storm-proof quarters gladly. Last night was wind still, however, and a beautifully clear, moonlit night, so that it was easy to see all over the area in front of us. My lads seem to be paying attention very well. With every instruction, I give the same sermon again: if any men approach, then let them come as close as possible so that we can get to grips with them. I visit my NCO stations every morning; one of the NCOs is in a Polish farmhouse, which is conspicuous because of the dirt. The other is living in a small wood in two huts we made which are half buried in the earth. The situation, the air, water and so on, make it seem as though the place is suitable for a country home; it's just a little bit out of the way.

My host, who owns a steam-powered lumber mill, which is not working at the moment, however, is called Rebbe and is what one would call in German a bekowet Jew. What a joy it was when I revealed myself to be a fellow Jew; he welcomed me with such friendliness; what gratification for them to pour out all their hopes and fears, and what joy for me to sit with them in the evening at the table and to feel a little bit as though I were at home. Here in the west, even the wealthier Polish Jews have a bad reputation; they appear to us to be arrogant and intrusive, but how different it is if one gets to knows them in their own milieu. Satisfied Jewish life pulsates together with rich, self-contained Jewish culture. The Jewish flavour which we try to find during our evenings at home, exists here. I wish that a merciful fate might make it possible for them to develop and give them strength for improvement and continue to see fulfillment and hope in their Judaism.

Yesterday evening, the people forgot their fear for once. Two girls, one of whom is known amongst the officers as the "beautiful Jewess" because of her fine, distinctive Jewish features, and their brothers sang Yiddish folk songs and songs of liberation. I knew some of the songs very well but others were new to me. I only regret that I cannot bring any of them back with me for you. A small two-year-old lad with a disarming, childish face, had learned a little of the text and melody to "Germany, Germany above all" and gave his all in singing it, much to my amusement. At the moment he is learning "The little birds in the forest" and so on, which his adult sisters learned from the soldiers marching through. At the end, the little one sang us a Jewish cradle song, and then he had to go to bed.

We sat together for a long time, and I will never forget this "cultural evening" in enemy territory.

Farewell.

Shalom and affectionate best wishes,

Your, Wertheim

A young rabbi – Knight of the Iron Cross.

A letter from senior physician Dr. N. to the Israeli Youth Association in Lörrach.
Near Ypres, 21st of November 1914.

I have just received the parcel of gifts dated the 21st of October. I was surprised and delighted by it in equal measure.

I see that the youth association doesn't forget its members even when they are on the battlefield. I am also convinced that every individual will do whatever is possible to make his association proud of him.

In future, no one will be able to say that we Jews went into this difficult battle as cowards. Yesterday, a major told me that the first Iron Cross in the battalion went to a young rabbi from Strasbourg, who had been unanimously recommended by his company.

A Jewish friend of mine, an NCO from Mülhausen, received not only the Iron Cross Second Class, but also the Iron Cross First Class. The common man or NCO only receives such an award for extraordinary acts of heroism.

Through its activities, our youth association has also educated its members to be men who are conscious of their duty towards their fatherland.

In this spirit, once again many thanks for the lovely things you sent.

With best wishes,

Dr. N., Senior Physician.

The kosher roast goose.

... During the march, I stopped a Russian farm wagon and bought a goose. Unfortunately, I didn't have a 25 Pfennig coin; it wouldn't have been much use to me anyway, because the Jew recognised me as a fellow believer and demanded 3 marks. We agreed on 2 marks. The news ran like wildfire through the column: A. has got hold of two geese, and I can already hear our senior lieutenant approaching at a gallop. "A., where are the beasts?" shouts the senior from 30 metres away. Lifting them up by the feet, I presented the white, feathered fellows to him, and delighted, he wanted to be the third one in the party; the second one was the staff sergeant, the "mother" of the column.

At the next stop, we grab hold of a Jewish man, and three minutes later, the fellows who are guilty of high treason are slaughtered according to strict ritual. As we marched into our destination, Olkusz, the senior lieutenant ordered quarters to be set up for me, and I had to be in charge of making roast goose. I soon found a Jewish family, who were delighted that I was also a Jew, and when I said that seven Jews had come with me, the bond of friendship was sealed.

But my God, the state of the kitchen: salon, living room and bedroom, tailor's workshop and kitchen all in one. One room with a bed was rented out. Well, I quickly cleaned up the stove, which wasn't easy because the family consisted of 14 heads, the smallest was 5 months old; it went on upwards to 21 years. The woman had the reputation of being a wonderful cook, following the basic rule that love goes through the stomach, and the husband had made this his motto. I left the feathers and giblets to the cook; the two stomachs were reserved for me.

Dinner was set for 9 o'clock, and the eight officers and five privates with the lieutenant at their head, gathered punctually. The rented room was quickly cleared for the purpose and the table beautifully decorated; everything was taken out of the cupboards, which made the people anxious. Our lieutenant was amazed at how I found my way around, and he had one surprise after another. He couldn't find words for it and just said, "Ah, ah", and shook his head. He had thirty bottles of beer brought over and the guard brought ten.

The two pretty daughters quickly washed their necks and hands, as they certainly needed to – cleanliness is frowned upon here! – tied on white aprons and began to serve. They began with the lieutenant with two plates that were passed on to the left and the right. Everything went wonderfully, and the atmosphere was charming. There were potatoes with hot goose fat poured over them, together with gherkins. A good peacetime meal, therefore, in the midst of the great tumult of war, in enemy territory, because barely 5 km away from our quarters, a Cossack patrol had been shot to pieces the day before.

The dressing station under shellfire.

A letter from Dr. Max Kirschner, son of Professor Kirschner, the first cantor of the Israeli religious community in Munich.

My telegram will probably have been in your possession long before this letter arrives. I have to give you more details about my being awarded the Iron Cross. I was dumbfounded when the captain told me yesterday that he had recommended me for an award having spoken with all the other officers, who had unanimously agreed with him. I was greatly surprised, and the decorations arrived in the evening; one Iron Cross was for me, the most honourable and sublime award that can be given to a soldier. I am to wear this medal, which I revered and of which I was always in awe. I was at the top of the company recommendations list; apart from me, the medal was given to the captain, the senior lieutenant and three NCOs. I was ashamed, in fact; I had the feeling that I had never done more than it was my duty to do.

I don't know whether I ever told you about the actions for which I have now been so honoured; because I received this medal, and this was pointed out specially, as a personal award.

I wrote to you about the bloody, appalling day, the 25th of August. The first reason for the award was that I kept a dressing station open all by myself under shellfire for three hours, taking care of about one hundred injured men. They were all from regiments other than my own, and their own doctors were not available. That was the first reason. Another reason given for the recommendation was: that upon arrival in the hell of ... in the pitch-black night, I went through the burning streets of the abandoned village with a patrol, managed to take care of six wounded Frenchman in a house, had them taken away as this house was also being shelled, and I was thereby able to help rescue these people. I found none of this to be anything special, but it was enough for the division to award me the Iron Cross. I gain particular satisfaction from the joy with which the officers ungrudgingly and without envy granted me the decoration and rejected my attempts to turn down the award, with assurances that I was fully entitled to wear the medal. As proof of their agreement, might I be allowed to say that we all addressed one another yesterday evening with the familiar "Du", even though I had only spoken openly about my religion for the first time the previous day. A wonderful sign, therefore, of togetherness and true comradeship.

World literature in jargon.

Skodnicki Duze near Lodz, 29. 11. 14.

Dear Schwabauch!

Today, it is possible for me to write to you in rather more detail. Yesterday, the post arrived again at last after nearly three weeks; amongst other things, a picture of dear Ida with little Hannah, just so sweet, a card from Alfred dated the 4. 11., a postcard from my dear mother dated the 14. 11. and two boxes from Käthe. Many thanks for those. So far, two parcel wagons for our troops have arrived with the columns. Three wagons with parcels are still standing in Kruschwitz. The post functions as badly as ever. I was lucky, however, because I received the letter from dear Ida dated the 2. 11. Johannisburg must look really bad. The Russians were there at the beginning of November and wreaked havoc. Even the Schencks fled to Königsberg. I expect that we will find nothing left of our flat and our possessions. But that is all right if we can see each other once more, fit and healthy!

30. 11. 14.

Our acetylene lamp went out yesterday, that's why I'm writing again today. You are happy that I still find the opportunity to satisfy my religious needs. Unless you are moving through Poland with your eyes closed, it is impossible to pass our fellow believers without seeing them. Last Thursday, for example, in ... I spoke to a fellow believer and asked, as I always do, whether I could eat kosher with him. So he took himself off to the head of the Jewish community. This well-educated man, as well-read in Jewish as in secular matters, came to our quarters immediately and invited me to come and see him. I couldn't accept accommodation from him, but I could accept an evening meal, and I spent several stimulating hours in his house. One of his sons is a sculptor and is studying in Paris; his daughter is studying music in Berlin. Nice young people who are loyal to their father's belief and yet thoroughly modern and well-educated. One finds it a lot in Poland, the drive for further education. In fact, I wrote to you on one occasion that in southern Poland in a little place called Tschedlowitz, I met young men and women amongst the ordinary people who discussed world literature in jargon and knew all about Shakespeare, Ibsen, Schiller, Goethe, Lessing etc. Many are Zionists. Each one of our fellow believers tells us the same thing: about the distress that they are suffering at the hands of the Russians. The Poles denounce the Jews, whom they associate with the Germans. The Poles paint white crosses on their own houses and put holy pictures in the windows so that they are immediately recognisable as non-Jews. Our people have already identified the Poles and my company in particular, has been well-informed by me.

I held a well-attended consultation in my room on Saturday, free of course. More than forty sick people with their relatives came to consult me. I also made a few visits. Great happiness in the town. And I was very satisfied. But one can do other things to help and be of use.

So, there you have another letter from me, and from it you have learned about the rather good side of life at war.

The mikveh as a public swimming bath for soldiers.*

On the battlefield, 3rd December 1914.

Dear Kurt!

I have been in a hospital in W. in Russian–Poland for three days; the reason was bronchial catarrh, but I am getting better and hoping to be able to return to the company very soon ... There are circa 4,000 to 5,000 Jews here in the town, out of 12,000 inhabitants, who are active primarily in trade and the restaurant business. I have found quarters with a rabbi, and I am, therefore, able to cast a glance into the life of our fellow Jews. Yesterday, I took a bath for the first time for many weeks; I could only find such a thing in the mikveh. It was, however, a spotless bath that refreshed me wonderfully. Beside the mikveh, there is a Beth HaMidrash where a kind of yeshiva is held. At home, in other words, with the rabbi, they learn shas. The fall of the voice, which we all know so well, will remain in my memory for a long time. A strange musical entertainment to accompany the good and inexpensive meals. Yesterday, I tasted the strange but very tasty broth called "borscht" for the first time. Today, Thursday, we are cleaning up for the Sabbath. And so one sees enough Jewish life in just a few days. If I were not so happy to be able to return to the front very soon, then I would regret not being able to spend the Sabbath here. It will be Hanukkah shortly. Keep well and think of our new Maccabees in Eretz Israel.

With cordial best wishes to you ... and to the Jewish Publishing House and to all in "Sächsiche Straße".

Your,
Theo Harburger.

The blood of the Maccabees.

6th of December 1914.

The parcel you very kindly sent to me was a pleasant surprise and I send my warmest thanks to the Jewish Gymnastic Club, including the third women's section, for the earmuffs they sent.

I also read the letter that came with it, with great interest; the Hanukkah celebrations that are so sublime for us will be felt more deeply this year by every one of us. We can happily confirm that Maccabee blood still runs through our veins, and every one of us carry out his duty and obligations and fight until his last breath. Even if many of us do not return, the blood in this war will not have flowed in vain, and the spirit will rise up anew. I am happy to tell you that I have already been in the thick of the fighting, and should it be God's will that I fall, then it is my wish that I may be able to keep fighting until the last battle in this war is over.

I would be very pleased to receive a general report from the gymnastics club from time to time.

With the loyal Jewish gymnastic greeting, and shouting a loud Hedad to all my dear gymnastic brothers and sisters, I remain,

Your,
Gustav Wolfermann.

Lacking ink and pen, I have to write this letter in pencil, I therefore ask you to please forgive me, and neither do I have a table so I have to use the ground. Best wishes once more.

Judah's struggle.

A letter from Landwehrmann Alfred Weil, 53rd Reserve Infantry Regiment.
Department of Oise, 7th December 1914.
19. Kislew 5675.

Dear Blue–White!

I was very pleased to hear from my fellow hiker Dr. Simon about the brisk, continued development of our idealistic efforts; I also hope from the bottom of my heart that we will come closer to our goal every day. Even though, during the course of this war, we shall probably have to mourn the bitter losses of dear fellow hikers, who will have died as heroes, then the rest of us, whose determination I do not doubt for a moment, will have to use twice our strength.

I am enclosing a small photo of a Jewish service that I attended yesterday afternoon at 3 o'clock together with 30 other comrades, in a schoolroom that had been set up especially for the occasion. The lectern was covered with a white cloth, and in front of it had been placed a pyramid of rifles surrounded by flower pots filled with sweet little indoor plants. The service was led by a very friendly rabbi from Berlin in the uniform of an army chaplain. Following on from the themes in the Torah, section 1. Book of Moses, Ch. 32, he spoke in depth about how Jacob patiently struggled with God and the people for many long years and finally, having been blessed by God with the name Israel, emerged victorious. So we, too, must bear the war imposed upon us by our enemies and the casualties, deprivations and exertions it brings with it, for our righteous battle must lead to the lasting peace for which Germany is ultimately fighting. We Jews have had to fight continuously for centuries against slanders that have been spread about us and our belief, and now Germany must, for a brief time, go through the same battle against the lies of the foreign press. It is now up to us Jews, who have to do more than our duty, just to exist, to improve our future situation through selflessness and the utmost devotion to duty, whereby each one of us will gladly contribute using all of his strength.

At the conclusion of the very moving address, we said our Mincha prayer with great fervency and prayed Kaddish for our brothers who have fallen on the field of honour. Our service was given a special consecration by the sound of artillery shells exploding nearby; they did not, however, cause any damage.

At the end, when the Sabbath was over, we wrote our own and our relatives' addresses in the chaplain's notebook and said goodbye to him in a warm and comradely manner with the thought that we had spent exalted hours together. We moved off in closed units and went back to our companies, some of which are scattered along the front lines.

I remain with cordial best wishes and Hedad,
Alfred Weil.

Chapter 4

"Yirah".

Bruß, 5 kilometres to the west of Lodz. 8. 12. 14.

My dearest uncle!

Yesterday, I was very happily surprised by your kind lines and the excellent cigars. I don't know which made me happier, the good cigars or your warm, good words; both show that you are kindly thinking about me and that feels good, especially in these serious times when those who belong together come closer to one another through inner need. When the days were quiet, I often thought about you, my dear uncle and you my dear aunt, and I felt how badly you were affected by Fritz's draft notice. Now I've heard, to my great joy, that he is already being trained to become an NCO, and it doesn't seem impossible to me that if he makes haste he can still become an officer.

So, we Jews see that we are being treated fairly at last, and we should not avoid any exertion or any sacrifice in order to reach this goal in a dignified manner. I am so very proud to be able to fight for our beloved, admirable fatherland. I am always aware that every Jew has a special responsibility to show that he is ready over and over again to give his life for the German cause and by doing so, proving the Jew's equality in his love for his fatherland.

As a German Jew, I have experienced strange things in this war through encounters with Polish Jews. The poor Polish Jew stands out from his Polish surroundings as though he is a different kind of person. He is not Polish as they are but German in his language and with all of his sensitivities. It was like a miracle to me when I came upon a Jewish family living amongst the squalid, filthy Polish peasant population. Whereas the peasants stubbornly hate the Germans and live in animalistic apathy and revolting filth, when I looked at the domestic life of the Jews, I undeniably became aware that something better, more noble, more ethnically valuable lives in the Jew which lends a purifying strength and blessing to his family life. I felt that the reason for this lay in the Jew's religion. Only his religion differentiates the Jew from the Pole. Where else could it come from, this difference between human beings? It is all too clearly evident between the Jew and the Pole, with whom the Jew shares all the living conditions of this wretched, miserable, pitiful existence. I was deeply moved at how the Jews practice their religion and recite the prayers handed down to them by their fathers, despite all the distress and danger; how only the Jews amongst the Poles keep the house clean and honour their women. That was "yirah"; it was an inherent natural decency. Here, I experienced the spirit of Judaism as a religion and its wonderful, purifying, ethical power. I saw it as my task to point out to my comrades this visible sign of a better human being so that I could work for the Jewish cause now, when everything feels more humane amidst the distress of war; first of all by continuously acknowledging that I am a Jew and at the same time by bringing them into closer human contact with Polish Jews.

I am experiencing great things at the moment: the Russians are fleeing in the direction of Warsaw. We're pursuing them, and their losses are appalling. But I have lost all pity for these animals, these herds of creatures. We Germans have to beat down on them without mercy, and we are doing that, thank God!

And now a cordial farewell! I send my warmest best wishes to you my beloved uncle and beloved aunt and embrace you with

sincere love.

Your loving nephew,

Kurt.

Preparations for the
Hanukkah celebrations.

From the letter from junior doctor Emil Salomon.
St. Juvin, 8. 12. 14.

... If we stay here, I hope to have a pleasant Hanukkah. Otto S. in M. was very kind to me yesterday and gave me 44 candles with tin holders together with matches so that I can light them each evening. On Saturday evening, the first evening of Hanukkah, I shall gather all the Jewish soldiers together here in my house. All in all there are about six of them; amongst them is a 23-year-old cantor, who was in Bingen before he came here. He found a chicken for me and killed it. Another Jewish musketeer, who used to be a cook in Paris, is going to prepare the tasty roast. I, as the big-wig amongst them, am going to take care of the wine and grog ...

The Kaiser on the front lines.

A letter from Reserve NCO Hugo Henle from Heilbronn, in the ...
Reserve Infantry Regiment.
D., 10. 12. 1914.

My dear friend!

I hope that my last card didn't give you a shock. You know, I have become nervous; it takes the character of a bear and nerves of steel to cope with all the things that I have seen and experienced. I still don't know if I have enough of either. The five months I have been at war have made me weary, and there are new impressions everyday which cannot be wiped away.

We were, and are, subjected to heavy artillery fire every day. A few days ago, a shell exploded five metres away from my window. Luckily, it didn't cause any damage. A day later, a piece of shrapnel flew through the window and lethally wounded our cobbler. Many of our comrades have also had to "bite the grass". We counted over 150 explosive shells and shrapnel shells falling to the right and left of us, in front and behind us. I am with the battalion staff, so I have to know our position and sketch it as well as the enemy positions; I would rather be in the trenches than in a house. As soon as it gets dark at about 4 pm, one has to be doubly careful and be ready to repel any night attacks by the enemy. We have all kinds of weapons for close-quarters combat; machine guns, spotlights, flares, hand-grenades, barbed-wire entanglements and ditches, bombs; devilish, murderous weapons which were still unknown even to our modern 20th century. Yesterday, a 21-cm howitzer was brought up to help keep the Russians away from us. Through repeated experience, I have realised that one must not underestimate the Russian, especially the way he digs in. The Russians entrench themselves in an incredibly short space of time and work their way forwards during the night by digging trenches which they connect with communication trenches. We disturb their work during the day by scattering artillery and machine-gun fire over the area as soon as we see anything. But at night, as soon as it is dusk, Russian labour battalions are driven forward – sometimes unarmed – and have to work their way up towards our positions. A small NCO post was recently forced back because it was attacked by superior forces, and when we drove the Russians back yet again two hours later, they were already finishing a 150 metre-long trench. They are 400 metres away from us but have the advantage of being able to call on support that is hidden behind trenches and communication trenches. As it is pitch black at 5 o'clock and the moon is waning, one has to be hellishly on guard. The Russians don't spare men; the poor men are driven forwards with the club if necessary. On top of that, Germany is presented to them as a country of barbarians on the lowest cultural rung, according to believable statements made by prisoners; they are told, for example, that all prisoners will be hanged on trees, that there is hardly one tree on which there is not a Russian hanging. The poor fellows believe it, of course, and when a Russian prisoner was led away yesterday, he trembled like an aspen leaf and cried until he confessed and we learned the things I have just written about.

One could write volumes about the trenches; we have turned into cave men, digging all day long. There are "villas" with names such as "Asylum for the Homeless", "Homeland Hostel" or "Luck in the Corner", one beside the other. Whatever furniture remains in the houses in the village is brought up – requisitioned is the correct military term for it – and we put our noses over the parapet as little as possible so as not to make the unpleasant acquaintance of the "blue beans". We live in the trenches all day long, and there we wash, though not always, receive gifts, take care of the necessary consumption of tobacco and alcoholic drinks, receive letters, parcels and newspapers, talk about the effect of our shells, undertake, if possible, a personal delousing; you dream about taking 83,625 Russian prisoners again, with you yourself fighting in the thick of the fray; the music plays a new national hymn, a drum beats up a storm and then another; then you get knocked by the man next to you who is stumbling out of the dugout towards the entrance to tell you that the enemy is firing again – so, the end of another dream.

Lighthearted and serious images alternate, unforgettable impressions that bear down on your spirit like a hundredweight.

I already wrote to you that I attended a service by Rabbi Dr. Sonderling from Hamburg; it truly was a beautiful, meaningful day. The way that he spoke to us was so simple, so apt and gripping that our hardened hearts became butter soft; but it was necessary, perhaps, and we all felt better afterwards. We spent the whole afternoon with Dr. S., and he told me about how many difficulties he had to overcome until he was not only authorised to become a chaplain but also appointed as one. There are 6 rabbis in the west and 2 in the east. Dr. S. has been assigned to the Army High Command. He wears a uniform, has the rank of officer, and he told me that after all kinds of difficulties he was now coping well with his duties. It must have taken a great deal of effort for him to stop eating kosher. But there are exceptions during wartime and one can't let oneself starve after all. Nonetheless, I hope to meet up with Dr. S. more often.

The Kaiser's visit here in the east went very smoothly. We were in the front rows and didn't get to see him; it has all been kept secret. A few men from each battalion were used – mostly decorated men – the condition was: a spotless uniform, spotless weapons etc. As I read through this order, I thought that something special must be happening, because this point was at the top of the divisional order. In D., which is behind this position, the men were paraded in front of the Kaiser, who was able to see for himself that his eastern army was in perfect condition – – –

I have already confirmed in a postcard that I received your last, kind letter of the 25. 11. I shall give your address to a comrade just in case. The temperature is very mild at the moment; the sun is shining as beautifully as it did in the autumn, and even if the tracks are just bottomless mud, this awful situation will soon be sorted out, too. I was very happy about the lines from your dear parents, so could you please thank them once again for writing, and send them my good wishes. If all of the large number of wishes being sent to me from all sides come true, then I may look to the future with a happy spirit. Until then, I will continue to carry out my duty for the good of my fatherland! So Heil and Sieg!

Greetings to everyone I know, your sister

and her husband and warmest best wishes to you, too.

From your devoted friend,

Hugo.

A comfortable house in the earth.

A letter from Isaak Meyer, a volunteer in a reserve battalion.
Firing position near B. B., 11. 12. 14.

Dear fellow gymnasts!

I thank you warmly for the kind letter and the gift. Those of us fighting in the war are very aware of the bonds that bind together all of us dear fellow gymnasts, but one is always very glad when a few lines bring back the memories of happy days. I have to say that the times I spent in the Jewish Gymnastics Associations, especially the time in the Cologne Youth Gymnastics Association, were amongst the best in my life. And as I walked through the streets of Lüttich to the German Governorate with a relatively small band of 42 people at the beginning of the campaign, similar feelings of pride moved through my breast then as they did when we performed in front of the public as Jewish gymnasts for the first time ...

We have made ourselves very comfortable here, as far as conditions and time allow. Yes, we have much more room out here with our guns than we usually get in our quarters. Our gun crew now has more than two bedrooms, half-buried in the ground, for four and five men respectively, a kitchen, a large living room and a shrapnel-proof dugout at its disposal. Now you are amazed! It's possible to build these kinds of constructions during a long siege. We consecrated the new living room yesterday evening. We had invited lots of guests. The place of honour along the side of the table was taken by our officers' representative. And 18 comrades slipped easily into the other places. There was enough to smoke and we didn't lack for drink. Our battery officer had brought the light we needed. Then we raised the roof. The house band started up. Do we have musical instruments? Indeed we do! A harmonica – a comb covered with greaseproof paper – two pieces of tin fixed to the stove served as drums; and with a little imagination one can imagine that a 96-pounder shell basket is a trumpet. The unwanted accompaniment to all of this was provided by the shells exploding nearby. To help you picture what our new home looks like, I want to tell you a little bit about it. First of all, we dug ourselves down quite deep into the earth, 2 metres deep. (6½ ft.) That cost us a few drops of sweat because of the stony, chalk ground, which already starts at a depth of 20 cm. So, the hole in the ground was 2 metres deep, 4.20 metres in length and 2.30 metres wide. The difficult part was covering such a large space. It sounds strange, but the French helped us. In the morning, I was wondering where to get the wood for it. Then, at midday, the familiar sound of shells hurtling over our heads. There was a mighty cloud of smoke half an hour behind us in C. Sometime later, we crept up to the town, keeping under cover, and instead of the beautiful pastor's house, we found nothing but a large heap of rubble. So then we got down to work! Wood; an abundance of the most beautiful beams. There were several large barn doors from another house that had been destroyed, and we moved off with all of that in a heavily laden wagon in the pitch darkness to our position in the fields. I was in charge of all the work, and it all went magnificently.

Now we are already sitting in our warm living room, and our spirits are high. The interior furnishings! A table, 2 ½ metres long and 1 metre wide, three benches, two on the long side and one on the upper narrow side. To the right, beside the expertly attached doors, is a small stove. There are a few wide steps, beautifully covered with wood, leading from the door up to the gun emplacement. Opposite the door up on the east side, half a window has been set up at a tilt. The whole thing is a glorious, light white. Now you are astonished again! Aren't you? We got hold of white bed sheets. They are stretched across the ceiling, and the material is pulled into a box shape every 60 cm. Behind the material on the walls and under the material on the benches, everything is stuffed beautifully with straw. The large white areas are discreetly enlivened by nails that are inserted into the walls every 50 cm through the stretched sheets. This is augmented by a length of black cloth that runs along below the ceiling along the walls. In the middle, the large table we made is covered with linoleum; in the evenings when we sit together in cosy companionship, it's covered in white, too. There is a nickel-plated lyre as a lamp holder. You'd be surprised, as well, if you could see this cosy home out in the middle of a field, invisible to the enemy. So, the time passes with shooting, working and sitting together in cosy companionship. Since the battles for B., we haven't been shooting very much. The French, however, fire enough shells for all of us. The amount of ammunition they use is quite astonishing. They "scatter" the whole area with shells of various calibres all day long. The shrapnel often flies around our heads. We've been in this position now for seven weeks, but the French haven't been able to find it, despite planes, tethered balloons and above all, despite the favourable terrain.

You may, perhaps, be interested to know how I get on with my comrades. I can only say that we get on magnificently together. I am the only Jew in the battery, and the only reservist in the gun crew. At first, I was with the baggage, but then, as soon as I made the request, I was sent to the gun crew. When the men then found out that I had volunteered to come to the front lines from the reserve battalion, they were more than friendly towards me. And now, with all the building construction around our gun, they all follow my command. The "Rundschau" is read by almost all of my comrades.

And now to your kind letter. You want to send more presents. First of all, I am not a heavy smoker, and then I think the right thing to do would be to make the appropriate resources available to our fellow Jews who have been driven from their land. Out here we have the opportunity to get to know the misery of those who have been driven from their homes. It does, indeed, look different than it appears in the illustrated papers. Not so picturesque. I wish you success in all activities. With sincere Jewish gymnastic best wishes.

Sincerely,
Isaac Meyer.

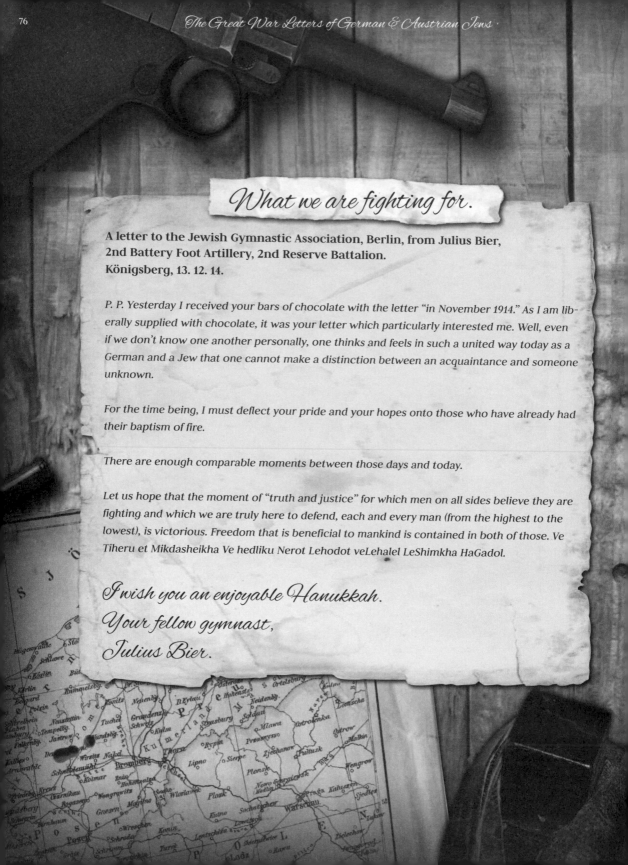

What we are fighting for.

A letter to the Jewish Gymnastic Association, Berlin, from Julius Bier, 2nd Battery Foot Artillery, 2nd Reserve Battalion.
Königsberg, 13. 12. 14.

P. P. Yesterday I received your bars of chocolate with the letter "in November 1914." As I am liberally supplied with chocolate, it was your letter which particularly interested me. Well, even if we don't know one another personally, one thinks and feels in such a united way today as a German and a Jew that one cannot make a distinction between an acquaintance and someone unknown.

For the time being, I must deflect your pride and your hopes onto those who have already had their baptism of fire.

There are enough comparable moments between those days and today.

Let us hope that the moment of "truth and justice" for which men on all sides believe they are fighting and which we are truly here to defend, each and every man (from the highest to the lowest), is victorious. Freedom that is beneficial to mankind is contained in both of those. Ve Tiheru et Mikdasheikha Ve hedliku Nerot Lehodot veLehalel LeShimkha HaGadol.

I wish you an enjoyable Hanukkah.

Your fellow gymnast,

Julius Bier.

C'est la guerre.

A letter from Corporal Wilhelm Glasfeld.
Zwevezeele, 13th December 1914.

Dear parents!

My first divine service in enemy territory. On the 11th of December at 2.50 in the afternoon, soldiers of Jewish belief gathered on the market square to go to divine service in the little town of Lichtervelde, 5 km away. Our battalion has only eleven Jewish soldiers including me, and how many there were in those days in the synagogue in School Street! We have been severely melted down. Punctually at 3 o'clock, we left the marketplace and marched for 50 minutes along the street towards Lichtervelde, a pretty little town: I already knew it because I marched through on the way here. When we arrived at the market place there, our commander, a 33-year-old volunteer, who is also a corporal, announced our arrival to the rabbi; the rabbi was from Magdeburg and was just getting out of his car. He wore an officer's coat with the Red Cross badge, and beside that there was a violet Star of David. He was a very nice man, and he talked to us for a while until the whole division arrived. Some comrades had covered 15 km to get to L. There were men from all branches and all ranks of the forces, and I met many old acquaintances. The commander of the town directed us to the meeting place and we went inside: there were about 100 men. The rabbi took two wine bottles instead of a candelabra, said: "C'est la guerre" and lit the Sabbath lights. Behind him was a little candelabra with the Hanukkah candles. Before the service began, each one of us filled out a form for statistical purposes for the Jewish community. We were asked to make a note on the back if we wanted a war prayer book or a Hanukkah booklet sent to us; I asked for both. Then there was one more question from a Jewish woman, who asked for addresses so that she could send gifts. And then we were asked if anyone knew how to recite prayers. A young man answered, and he had a splendid singing voice. First of all there was an introductory prayer, then Lecho dodi (Hebrew, Ashkenazic pronunciation, meaning "Come my beloved", used in the Sabbath liturgy - ed. note) and then Shema Yisrael as it is sung in your synagogue at home. Then came the address. The rabbi reminded us about the Friday evening celebrations when we sit with our loved ones and candles are lit. Then the Hanukkah lights were lit and we sang "Under your protection" in Hebrew as we used to at home with father. Afterwards, the rabbi gave a wonderful explanation about what the words mean and how this song is so appropriate for the present time. Then we sang L'chu, n'ranenah ("O come, let us sing" (landonai - unto the Lord), the wine was blessed and then came the Kaddish for those who mourn. Finally, he blessed us, and we marched along the pitch-black road back to our quarters, which we reached at 7 o'clock. It was beautiful; I wish there was a service every Friday. Admittedly, the Hanukkah lights were lit one day too early, but we did at least get to see them. The next day, the rabbi had to be with the ... Division, otherwise the service would have been one day later. Of course, he chose lovely words to remember those who had fallen, those who were prisoners and wounded.

Your loving son, Wilhelm.

The first little light ...

A letter from Reserve NCO Eugen Seelig, Mannheim. (See "A Meeting.")
Currently at P.-à-V., 14th December 1914.

My dear Doctor!

*I received your last post and newspapers, and I thank you warmly for all your good wishes
and for all your efforts.*

*I expect that your Hanukkah celebration yesterday was a very happy one; I thought of you all a lot.
Unfortunately, the unfavourable conditions prevented me from holding a celebration with a larger
number of people, as I had intended, so that on Saturday evening I only had the company of one
Jewish comrade, with whom I lit the first little light in my quarters. (I had, in fact, received a parcel
from our rabbi with ca. 40 proper Hanukkah wax candles.) Because I didn't know the text of "Ma'oz
Tzur" from memory, we sang a song from our army prayerbook, the text of which was rhythmically
appropriate to the melody of "Ma'oz Tzur". The next day, yesterday that is, I sent a man on a bike
to Rabbi Dr. Chone, who at the moment is quartered in M. about 3 km from here, and I asked him
for the "Ma'oz Tzur". He tore the appropriate pages out of his prayer book and sent them to me
with a very friendly accompanying letter. I had invited a few Jewish comrades who were available
in the evening. There were four of us altogether. We lit our little lights at about 8:30 and began our
Ma'oz Tzur Yeshuati, followed each time by the appropriate German verse. Joy radiated on all faces
and everyone was taken over by the feeling that we belonged together. There were two ordinary
young people who didn't have much connection with national Judaism and Zionism but who knew
the melodies of the brachot before the lighting up, etc. (even better than me). Thanks to the gifts
that you and other dear ones sent me, I was in a position to feed them with lots of chocolate,
cigarettes, cake and confectionery, and so we stayed together for another two hours, conversing
(mostly about Jewish matters) in a very lively fashion! Then we parted in the knowledge that we
had celebrated our Hanukkah far from all our loved ones as well as the conditions allowed. We
promised one another to meet in the evenings as often as possible to light our little lights. I ask you
to give my best wishes to all the dear Blue-Whites. To you particularly, warmest regards,*

Your,
Eugen Seelig.

Hanukkah on the battlefield and at home.

A letter from Leo Cohn of the 28th Reserve Infantry Regiment to the directors of the Jewish Walking Club "Blue-White" in Mannheim.
Savonières, 19. 12. 14.

Dear Dr. Simon!

Above all, many thanks for your parcels and newspapers. I am in the best of health. We have just returned from the trenches, soaked and filthy; we took off our backpacks and weapons and ate something whilst the post was being distributed. Thoughts of best wishes from home help us over many difficult hours.

You can probably imagine that we were filled with joy when we unpacked the Hanukkah candle-holder with the candles. The Hanukkah celebrations have never made such an impression upon me as they did this year in battle. We can look back with pride to the deeds of our Maccabees, and hopefully we will have got rid of the slander about our cowardice and the assertions that we Jews are unfit for a military career.

Now I want to continue by telling you how Polde and I celebrated Hanukkah. At dusk we lit our little lights according to the ancient customs, in the circle of our non-Jewish comrades, who observed our Hanukkah candleholder with reverence. I explained a little of the significance of our celebration to them. I feel great attachment towards the Jewish race at such times as this. The campaign will hopefully have shown that we Jews born in Germany are also good Germans.

Poor Fritz Seelig! He, too, belongs to those brave men who died for the fatherland. Why did you not tell us that? There were many comrades who fell beside us. How will that look to our leadership! God will surely spare us further gaps. Kahnheimer wrote to me about your Hanukkah celebrations in Hemsbach. How beautiful it must have been in your house. But the way we feel about this Hanukkah celebration, the childish joy with which we lit the candles – it was a sublime moment. Today, we are going to light the eighth little light; our thoughts are with all of you, our dear ones at home.

We hope that the Hanukkah celebrations will have brought a turning point, that our enemies, like the enemies of Judah, will be punished for their insolent presumptuousness.

We send best wishes to you and all the Blue-Whites. Enos and Polde.

Chapter 5

The Sabbath in Poland.

**A letter from Max Marcus, NCO in the ... Reserve Infantry Regiment.
In the trenches near Kielce, 11th January 1915.**

Beloved mamma, dear brothers and sisters!

Even though I need to reply to many people's letters, I really want to write to you again in more detail. Today, I'm also looking back on a year of life. It will remain unforgettable for me with its great experiences and its terrible impressions. I will remain eternally thankful to you all for your great, deep love, which you all show towards me constantly, and with which you have all eased a particularly terrible time for me and so often embellished it. May I be lucky enough to return to you in the new year fresh and unscathed after a victorious and happy end to the campaign; I shall know how to thank the Almighty for his merciful protection and you, for your deep love and loyalty.

And now I'll give you a little insight into life and activities, my feelings and thoughts out here.

It was last Friday evening; I had just greeted the beloved Sabbath out in the forest, the melodies from home transported me back to the dear prayer house at home, and in high spirits I ended my prayer. I went through the trenches to the dugout and crept in, because it's only 1¼ metres high. How happy I would have been if a like-minded comrade had come towards me and taken my hand for a Sabbath greeting. But instead of the lightness of the Sabbath house, which would have corresponded to my inner state, I found everyone asleep in the darkness. Some of my comrades were crouching at the stove frying potatoes, the others, who had only just left the guard posts, lay resting or sleeping in the corners. I felt a painful tension inside. All my thoughts flew to you, my dear ones, who will also be thinking of me over here this evening and like me, longing for the Sabbath evening that lights up our house and our hearts with the beams of the Sabbath light and fills them with the joy of the Sabbath peace; it gathers us around you, beloved mama, safe and happy. I imagine it all to be so beautiful; how thankful I would be to enter the prayer house again, how happily all of us who are fighting for the security of our homeland would stretch out our hands in greeting, how festively my dear parents' house will radiate on this evening. But the realisation of this hope dwells in the far distant future. The wind is still whistling around our little dugout window; it sweeps over the water that forms into lakes on the meadows and marshes around our position after snow and rain. It is also one of the reasons that everything in front of our front lines has been quiet for days, for who could hope to advance here. Even the artillery guns have to remain silent, because they can't find their objectives in this murky weather. (Today, Monday, in the clear weather, our heavy artillery lay down a heavy barrage and set fire to the town of Lopuschno, which lies directly behind the Russian lines.) Fearfully, we all ask ourselves the question: how much longer? Our task is difficult. On Friday evening, this question oppressed me a great deal, and on top of that, we've had no post for eight days because of the impassability of the roads. And now, in addition to the fear, comes the anxiety about your welfare. So one thought followed the other, one memory, one longing. My thoughts remained hanging on one Friday evening that I had in Poland, and I wished that it could soon be like that again if I can't be at home for the moment. It was on the 21st of August, on your birthday dear B.: we arrived in Tuschin, near Lodz. There were a lot of Jews living in the town. In the afternoon, I looked around inside the synagogue and then visited it at school time. I found it closed, however. I went back into the street. A Jewish woman looking out of the window explained to me that, because of the war, the service was being held in a neighbouring house. Soon, I was standing there amongst the people who were praying, having being guided through yards that led into one another, and I was announced with the comforting remark: "A soldier, a Yid." They had just come to the loud Shmoneh Esreh. (Shmoneh Esreh, "the eighteen", referring to the original number of blessings; it is the main prayer in the Jewish liturgy - ed. note.) This had barely finished when they all came towards me with a hearty "Shalom aleichem." After the ritual, we prayed. At the end of the service, people were almost tearing each other to get at me, everyone wanted to have me as a Sabbath guest. I would have preferred to follow the man and woman who had pointed out the way to me. Their Sabbath room was light and clean, their table was festively decorated; I imagined that a Friday evening in this house would be atmospheric. I submitted to the Elder, of course, and at his instigation I followed a man who, during the week, had returned from his conscription. On the previous Sabbath, he had been far away from his family, far beyond Warsaw. Luckily, he had been released from duty and had vowed to have three soldiers at his table if possible the following Friday evening. So I came along just at the right time. I entered his house; he was happy to be able to fulfill his Neder, and in this small cottage, I was pleased to observe the good fortune and joy of the man who had returned unexpectedly. (A Neder is a declaration, using God's name, accepting a self-made pledge, stating that the pledge must be fulfilled. It may be to fulfill a future action or to refrain from some action - ed. note.) It was such a completely different Sabbath for these people than the last one had been. He entered the narrow, brightly lit Sabbath room as though he had been blessed. He blessed his 6 children, and he and his wife welcomed me warmly. As small as the cottage was, everything was there for everyone in abundance: Matzos were brought for both of us, and an abundance of good food came to the table from the family's kitchen. We exchanged experiences at the table; he talked about the difficulties of Russian conscription, because many conscripts didn't know exactly where they had to present themselves or were not named in the lists of the area command to whom they had been ordered. So a lot of time was wasted; in the meantime, we Germans entered the country, and many men were relieved of their duty to sign up because they were, of course, not allowed through by us. I, too, had seen and experienced a lot of things in these first two weeks of the war; so the conversation was very stimulating.

After the meal the neighbours arrived; they wanted to greet the man who was now happily back at home and me. I would have liked to have stayed, but duty called. I promised to come to the service, and at his insistent request, to a midday meal if at all possible, next day. In any event, he gave me food in abundance to take with me; the man was so happy that he had been able to carry out his Neder so quickly. That has been the only wonderful Friday evening in battle up until now. I haven't been able to spend a Sabbath morning in a community. Early next morning, we, that is, the 1st Battalion, were put on alert. The ethnic Germans in Lodz had asked for German protection. The 2nd Battalion was sent there in a hurry on hay wagons, whilst we stayed at an outpost facing Lodz. So the Sabbath joy was lost for me.

So thinking about the future and the past, I sat quietly in a corner. Then the dawn came: the field kitchen arrived and the men were fetching their food. I, however, pulled out of my pocket a well-preserved envelope and took out your splendid photo, beloved mama, with little J. on your lap and E. in the background, which you, dear E., had sent to me together with the delightful picture of your dear children. I looked at the beloved, precious faces with great emotion and ardour and felt myself to be closer to you. I looked at them for a long time, and my thoughts dwelt on the happy pictures for a long time, imagining my happy return to you. I ate supper, as far as my food stocks allowed it, and then I went to bed early, on the straw.

I assume that such an atmospheric picture from the battlefield interests you; but I have to stop for today. I will write to you as soon as possible about my observations in Koniecpol, about the suffering and pain of our fellow believers; also about the destruction of the houses and possessions which the peasants and property owners have had to put up with and which have turned Poland into a completely impoverished country for years to come.

For today, I send my love to you all, with heartfelt thanks.
From your devoted,
Max.

At the front lines.

A Letter from Hugo Henle from Heilbronn … Reserve Infantry Regiment. Braunsberg, 27. 1. 1915.

My dear friend!

I have received your kind letter of the 24th of the month and want to answer it immediately.

I have let it be known that I intend to return to my old unit – to the battalion – after my convalescence, and my lieutenant and battalion adjutant wrote to me recently explaining how I can make this happen. They would all be pleased if I returned, and I think that I prefer this to your suggestion of having myself transferred to a Landsturm regiment. I am not that ill, and I would very much like to return to the old unit – I like being there, and up until now I haven't been hit by a bullet, and if I continue to stand under the protection of our all-bountiful God, he will continue to watch over me and protect me in the hour of danger. But, dear Theo, I have the feeling that at the moment, at this hour when the fatherland is in danger, every Jew must stand firm and do more than is required, more than duty demands!

Having become aware of the great honour of fighting victoriously on the front lines for my precious fatherland, I shall be on the front lines afterwards to join in when the call comes to stand up for equality for our fellow believers in all walks of life. These motives induce me not to spend the present battle for our existence, behind the lines. I am fighting, as is every German, and I fight so that afterwards I can stand up as a German for the rights of German Jews. Perhaps we can talk about this subject together another time.

I will certainly still be here for the rest of the week and your news will still reach me. I thank you warmly for the letter from Dr. W. that you sent to me. All my love to your dear parents as well as your sister and brother-in-law, and I embrace you.

From your devoted friend,

Hugo.

Prepared.

A doctor from Frankfurt wrote to his parents from the battlefield.
D..., 21st of January.

My dear ones!

I have just recited the Maariv prayer and in an atmosphere of devotion still, I am now reading your letters ... Also, your dear, good words, dear father, do me good, with the constant reference to one beautiful Jewish sentence. Particularly because I am so alone here as a Yehudi, and because with the duties I have I am confronted with so many difficulties, I especially understand the significance of the words Zedoch tazil mimowes; yes, the fulfillment of duty that God looks for and finds, even if the circumstances are as unfavourable as can be. Duty breathes a sigh of relief when, despite everything, the daily mitzvahs are fulfilled. These protect us from a spiritual, ethical death, which is a thousand times worse than physical death, from becoming animals, brutalised, degenerate. And so, I am overjoyed and content every day when I put on the tefillin, when I can recite my morning, midday and evening prayers at the right time. And what on earth would my comrades say if they discovered my tefillin in my bread bag one day, and I explained to them that they belong to my daily needs just as much as bread does ...

We are expecting a French attack tonight, everyone is at his post, our dressing station has already been set up, the air is humid ready for a storm and it's totally quiet outside. I hope it doesn't happen, because however it ends it will not take place without casualties, and at the moment, I am the only doctor in the battalion. The medical officer is ill. Before you get these lines, you will be able to read in the newspapers whether an attack took place or not.

If these lines reach you then it will, perhaps, be Chamisha Asar; this time it falls on Sabbath Shirah! How strange; will the coming spring allow us to sing the shirah, soon as well? God grant it ...

Atmospheric images from Poland.

A letter from Max Marcus NCO in the ... Reserve Infantry Regiment
(See "The Sabbath in Poland.")
Kraszuszinm, 18th January 1915.

Beloved mamma, dear brothers and sisters!

This afternoon, most of the men in my room have gone on guard duty, so I want to use the truly beneficial calm to tell you about my experiences and impressions in Koniecpol.

On Saturday evening, the second day of Christmas, I was summoned by the sergeant who showed me the battalion's orders: "The 1st company will prepare four horses, a wagon, and commander of transport NCO M., who is to report to the battalion-office at 7.45 in the morning, to pick up the post in Koniecpol." I was glad to take over this commission. Even if our brigade in Chastkow was miles away, we were still lying squashed in beside one another like herrings in the peasants' impoverished, filthy houses. The daily drill could be enjoyed for a week, but it had also lost the attraction of novelty. So I was very happy to have the opportunity for once to go on an excursion and see what it was like behind the front lines. In the morning, I arrived punctually: my wagon drawn by four horses, with two seats and with a heavy sheepskin on them for me, together with one wagon with two horses from each of the other battalions, were already standing ready. The battalion adjutant gave me the route and various errands to run, the battalion commander ordered me to come back as quickly as possible. Both of them wished me bon voyage and off I went. The 1st and 2nd company were standing all along the village street, occupied with repairing the terrible road. Many officers gave me a hearty sendoff; each one of them wanted something. Cognac, rum, candles, tobacco, cigars, matches, petroleum; it felt as though I were going off to a different world. We had not long left the village when we noticed that something was wrong with the four in hand, the horses were not used to one another. So we stopped by the next farmhouse and requisitioned a wagon. I continued with four wagons. I firmly intended to give the wagon back to the farmer on the return journey, of course. The way home, however, didn't take me back that way, because the regiment had advanced, and so, unfortunately, the farmer didn't get his wagon back. It will not be the last in this year to be taken from his house without payment.

At about 2 o'clock, I arrived at the first small town, Szeczemin, having travelled over roads that were in fairly good condition. I was given the location of a Jewish house in which I could eat; as a Jew, I was taken in warmly and given excellent food, a good midday meal at a Jewish table. I continued my journey after an hour; this last part was the worst, and it took four hours to cover just 10 km until we arrived in Koniecpol in pitch blackness. The road was appalling; the horses sank up to their knees in mud and had to strain terribly to pull the empty wagons forwards. But it's hardly a surprise that these terrible roads become bottomless in bad weather, because they are used so much. Two powerful armies have marched along it many times, and now, one column after another moves along this road to Koniecpol, with 4, 6, 10, 20 wagons, to fetch ammunition, provisions, food, post and so on for the troops stationed behind it; these then drive back the same way heavily loaded.

Koniecpol is a little town the size of Pinne (formerly in Prussia, now Pniewy, Poland – ed. note) with quite a large marketplace. In the middle of that is the quartermaster's store where the food is stocked. Close to the marketplace there are row upon row of German and Austrian troop columns standing beside and behind one another. The commissariat was in the Koniecpol theatre, so I was told by the superintendent, which was where I was given oats for my horses; the ammunition depot is outside the town, of course. The town has about 1,500 Jews and 1,000 Poles. As I already told you, I found shelter for the wagon, the horses and the driver immediately, then went to the area command office. The sergeant there fed me well with cognac, eggs and bread rolls, and then gave me a quartermaster's note for the field post. I was quartered there with the postillions, who proved to be very comradely. They had plenty of blankets and furs and gladly gave me some of them so that I was able to pack myself up well and was able to sleep well on plenty of straw in a comfortable room. I can't remember what it's like to sleep in a bed, and during the last 5½ months, I have only had that pleasure in Wreschen and Pabianice. The straw bed on the earth suits me well, thank God. I only need to be underneath a warm roof and I am very happy.

Next morning, I got up in time and had myself taken to the shul; it was in darkness, however, they were praying in the Beth HaMidrash. I was observed curiously, almost fearfully, at first; only when I took out my tefillin did everyone calm down and was happy. One thing agitated me greatly; apart from a few people, everyone walked around the almemor, (the place in a synagogue from where the Torah is read), which I felt caused a lot of disturbance during the service. When I asked if this and also smoking cigarettes, which people did now and again, was usual in the shul, as well, it was explained to me that it was only allowed here. But apart from this, I felt so happy and so at home to be able to pray once more in a house of prayer in a large community. How close I felt to these poor Jews, who have to cope with distress and danger because of their faith in these difficult times. Then I was allowed to go up to the Torah – it was Monday – and moved and grateful, I was able to praise the All Bountiful One, who had until now, guided me so mercifully, and through his Torah had anchored trust and hope in me so strongly. After the service, several people came up to me to greet me. Here, as in all larger communities, the prayers continue until midday, with those who arrive later always waiting until the end and then uniting to form a new minyan. As I was crossing the market square after the service, a whole company had lined up; not soldiers, however, but mostly Jews, young and old, and Poles, armed with spades, pickaxes and similar tools. I immediately made enquiries about the reason for this gathering and was told that every house had to provide one man to repair the roads each morning. On Wednesday morning I went to the shul. A murmur went through the rows. I heard something about an order from the area commander. After the service ended, the venerable rabbi went to the almemor and announced: "Because many of you have avoided working on the streets by going to the Beth HaMidrash until midday and have stated this as the reason for not being able to work, the area commander has ordered that the service in Beth HaMidrash must finish at 8 o'clock, and the evening service may not begin before 6 o'clock, except on Friday evening when it may begin at 4 o'clock." Now there was no escape, because no one could leave the town without a stamped pass.

Almost every Jewish house has become a tea room in which very good tea can be had for 10 Pfennigs a glass. Women or children stand in front of the door and invite you in, in a friendly manner; so I followed the invitation of a darling little girl and had a very stimulating evening in her house. I was interested in hearing more about the Jews' situation from her father, and I was able to learn a thing or two. All trade in Poland, of course, was entirely in the hands of Jews, as it used to be in Posen. That ended last year. With the support of money from Polish magnates, banks and associations, Poles have begun to stand on their own feet, as is happening in Germany, so that some cooperatives are already buying everything from the farmers, supporting them financially, and so, in many cases, excluding the Jews. Businesses are opening up in other branches, too, to the detriment of the Jews. Thanks to their freedoms, there are more possibilities for Jews in Germany to start a new life somewhere else. Here in Poland where poverty and overpopulation are the same everywhere, it is much more difficult to do that, and so, slowly, even greater poverty is appearing. In Koniecpol, the food shops are doing good business, of course. They can get rid of their goods easily because of the heavy military traffic going through. The prices are high: crushed sugar 50, cubes 60, candles 1.20, petroleum 50, although it must be noted that a Russian pound and hundredweight are only a little bit more than three quarters of a German pound and hundredweight respectively. The craftsmen are suffering particularly badly from the war, of course. The tailors, cobblers and so on, but also the manufacturers. That's the difference in Germany; there, the poorer people have stronger purchasing power, because of state support and wages sent home. In Poland, the land has been destroyed, the farmer impoverished, the soldier is given a minimum wage from which nothing is left over. Many people attempt to make up the difference by selling tea, bread rolls, cake and cigarettes, people who would otherwise have nothing to do with selling; trade is not bad, however.

A one-off tax is fixed once a year by a government commissar, who comes into the shop, looks around and then determines the amount. Apparently, many stocks become remarkably small on those days. As in all things, the ruble plays a large role, apparently.

Conditions in the schools are very bad. Most children go to the cheder, and there they learn the things that belong to their Jewish education. Unfortunately, the rabbi, an older gentleman in poor health, is no longer capable of participating in the education of the young people. I heard contradictory things regarding permission to attend high school. It doesn't look as though it will happen any time soon, and the demand for it doesn't seem very great; the desire for it and for more advanced education and culture don't seem to be exceptionally great. When I asked, for example, why most people wear their tzitzit hanging out from under their waistcoats, why they all still wear the long coat and the typical Jewish cap, were they forced to do so, I was given the answer: father does it like that and grandfather, as well, so we are doing it, too. The day of liberation from the Russian yoke would probably change a lot of things.

Before I leave the Jews, I must mention a happy observation. In shul during prayers, I saw two young people zealously engrossed in the Gemoro; I was very pleased. At the midday meal, I met a young girl. When I asked her who her fiancé was, she answered me proudly: a Gemoro boy. And what would you live from, I asked her? Well, he still has a good business. This answer pleased me even more. As long as this race has such young men at its centre, who do not neglect to study the Torah alongside their profession, as long as its daughters are proud of these men, then the good religious kernel of the race will be preserved; it still thrives beneath life's waste. May the day of liberation come very soon for these poor people, may that bright day find a religious, robust race.

And so now I have to come to an end. You know how I got hold of my post. On the return journey, I passed whole rows of injured men from whom I learned that our regiment was engaged in fighting. I almost felt as though I had forgotten my duty, having spent pleasant days here whilst my comrades found themselves in a hail of fire. On Friday afternoon on New Year's Day, I arrived in Krassuszin – along the way, I had been told where the regiment was stationed; there, I heard that the regiment had been engaged in fighting again and I had to wait there. The post had to wait there, too. The paymaster came towards me, and I have seldom seen such great joy as when he saw the large amount of post. He almost fell around my neck with joy. Distribution of the post to the companies began immediately, under my supervision. It was a lot of work. Then, at dusk, it was time to go to my company. During the night, they and the battalion had come to within 400 metres of the Russian positions. Shortly after they had dug themselves in, the Russians noticed them and began to direct heavy fire at them. They came under heavy fire again early the next morning, when they withdrew because the Russian positions were too strong. Four men were killed in our company. Three were wounded. I met my comrades in the trenches, at an outpost; everyone was overjoyed; we have now been here for fourteen days.

Enough for now. I send you all my love.

Your devoted Max

A surprise attack.

Souain, 22. 12. 1914.

Thank God I am still alive and unhurt, whereas many, many of my men, all of them, in fact, who were near me during yesterday's attack by the French, are dead or injured. So once again; 1. Manie, so that you're not worried, I need nothing whatsoever, and I am still in the trenches. The story is actually too appalling to describe, but how I alone escaped with my life and unscathed, only because of divine providence, is inconceivable to me. It was 10 o'clock in the morning and the company wages were being handed out. As usual, I took the money that the men wanted to send home, when, suddenly, the French attacked us with the most appalling artillery and rifle fire. I rushed back through the trenches to my dugout, put on my backpack, fetched my rifle and fixed my bayonet. We were not able to stay crouched down there for long but jumped up and over towards the left where there was more cover. Ten minutes later we had to move to the right again, back to our previous position so that we could fire on the French, who were advancing. At the same moment, a hailstorm of shells and shrapnel came down on top of us. The air pressure blew me onto the ground, and I was buried by the collapsing earth so that only my head was sticking out. Hands, arms, everything was trapped, and I had to endure in this terrible situation for an hour whilst the shells exploded close by me continuously, injuring many of the men. I screamed at the men who came along in between and wanted to dig me out, telling them that they should clear off and get themselves to safety. It is inconceivable to me and to everyone here how I escaped with my life in this way. I was absolutely ready for death and was waiting for the end. When I was dug out later, I touched myself everywhere, but I was alright, there was just one lens broken in my spectacles, which I carry in my backpack, and my pince-nez was badly bent. But I can't tell you what it looked like all around me! I will never be able to forget the sight, and the general opinion is that this was the worst day that the regiment had experienced since the beginning of the war. But this is the main thing; sadly, amongst the many men who were killed, there was also a Jew who belonged to my group. He was called L. L. and was the son of the widow B. L., who also has four or five other sons on the battlefield. One of them, who was initially reported missing, had been injured and then captured by the French. For me, it is a very sensitive matter to write all of this to this woman, and I ask you, dear Manie, to give this mission to Dr. C.; Dr. C. will certainly be prepared to inform the woman, I thank Dr. C. warmly for that. L. was much loved amongst his comrades. He had already been injured once. Fortunately, he was dead immediately; in other words he felt no pain. We buried them all that night. With the exception of L., who has a grave for himself, they are all lying in a mass grave. Altogether, there are ten men from our company. Afterwards, as soon as I've finished this letter, I shall make a Magen David (the Shield of David, more commonly known as the Star of David; a relatively new Jewish symbol intended to represent the form of King David's shield - ed. note) for the grave, out of wood. I shall also go to the service at dawn tomorrow morning at Somme-Py and ask Rabbi Dr. Levi to deliver a eulogy. Please tell all of this to the woman to comfort her. But please do not say that one son is a prisoner of war as I don't know if the woman already knows this. Also, all this information ought to be given to her on the same day that you get this letter, before her son's letters come back marked "fallen". I took his letters, watch and chain and 5.20 Marks from him, and they will be sent off the day after tomorrow. I shall distribute any parcels that might come for him, to the needy. It was terrible work, dragging the wounded away and bandaging them. We brought in two Frenchmen in the evening, as well, and bandaged them. One of them was a poor devil of 35 years with 4 children. I can mark the 21st of December in red on my calendar, and I can't thank God enough for my wonderful rescue.

A "decent" piece of shrapnel.

POSTKARTE.

ostcard from J. J. Dorusz, an infantryman in the
stro-Hungarian Army.
e original was written in Yiddish.

aise be to God! Motzei Shabbos Kodesh.
dolf Hospital.

reetings to you my dear Elias!

ough I find it rather difficult to write because my hand is
trembling, as you will see from this letter, I will give myself
ish and force myself to get out of bed in order to send my
t wishes you, Elias, because I am so happy to have received a
er from you. From this I see that you are taking extraordinary
e of "Yisroel's" soul. I have never been to Russia. I travelled
Rzeszow, Glogow, Ropcze, Debica, Pilzno, Czarno, Tarnow,
omysl, Mielec, Majdan, Bojanow and Nisko. In Nisko I got
share, namely a decent piece of shrapnel during an attack;
n the lung, prost, cheers! After lying there unconscious for
hours, I wanted to see if I was still alive. I crept slowly to a

stretcher, on which I was brought to the dressing station. Then
I was in Tarnobrzeg for 12 days, and finally, I came here. Here
they thought about it: A mere shot in the lungs is too little – and
I had been operated upon, too, but that wasn't so bad, thank
God. I am doing well, God be praised. It is already healing. Now,
I only have one tube inside instead of the original two.

I have heard nothing from my dear wife until now. I only
received a letter from Chaim Berisch today. Thank you very
much for your lines, for that is my only pleasure here.

Your Jisroel Jaakauw.
Best wishes to your revered father and all
of his relatives, and each one individually.

Photographie, Druck und Verlag von E. Prietzel. Steyr. 1914

"Revenge for Kishinev".

A letter from an infantryman in the Austro-Hungarian Army, Chaim Ohrgut.
The Yiddish original was written with Hebrew lettering. The transcription is
based on Galician pronunciation.
(The English translation follows the Yiddish original).

Burchhaschem b'machne hazowu dalet marcheschwen tar ajin hei.

Jdidi chawiwi k'nasschi. Leib'sch!

*Jo Brieder, ch'leb tchias hameissim ofgetannen, 6 Misleß gelegen innem finsteren
naßen Keiwer, haint werd es Schitzengraben geriefen, in bin Widder megilgel geworen
bei hachajim, ober mein nicht, as idi schmies eppes chochmes, s'is heint nicht die Zeit
davin. Vor'gen Donnerschtig bin ich arein in Schizengraben, hob gelanzt in geschossen,
geschossen in frisch gelanzt, a bissel gerastet in widder poj, schajns hob ich noch gehatt,
wus ich hob bei mir in Bisem getrugen das Fläschele Cognak, wus die host mir far etliche
Wochen geschickt. Ch'hob mir gekeent a bissel den Giemen benetzen in mit neiem Mut
die Awoide tien.*

*Jo, gitter Brieder, Ich leb, main inssane toikew hat mir far dos mul noch zim gitten
ingeschrieben, ober doch is mir dus Harz of Sticker zerrissen, here aus a Geschichte a
rihrende, überhaput far dir: far 2 Wochen hobben mir gehatt Sturmangriff in neben mir
is demmelt gestannen a schwarz cheineddiger Sellner, ausgesehen a Ungar, wus is mir
schojn oft durch sein Ofnotieren stets wehrend der Pausezeit, in a klein Notizbiechel,
offallend gewesen, s'is ober demmelt kain Zait gewesen Bekanntschaft ze machen, me hot
befoilen stirmisch vorzegehen, ch'hob die schojn amul beschribben wie asoj dus auseht,
in du her ich a Kritz mit die Zajn vin main Schuhen in a Brimm zi: "Rache far Kischinew", in
dus eidele milde Punim hot bekimmen a ziere vina Bestie. Der Sturm hot gedauert b'erech
5 Schu in mir hobben den Fain vin a wichtige Stellung vertribben, die ganze Nacht hot
men schojn of dem Kampffeld gerastet, se morgens her ich wie me schmiest eppes mit
Staunen in Wunderung vin a jiddischen Kapral wus er hot beim nächtigen Sturmangriff
dem Oberleitnant vina sicheren Tojd gerettet, dus Leben vim Oberleitnant hot gehongen
of a Hur, 2 Kosaken hobn ihm mit ihre Pickes attackiert, in de jiddische Kapral hot ihm
durch 2 geschikte Hiebe of die Kosaken mazel gewen. Ich hob nuch dem Numen vin'm
Kapral geforscht in erfahren, (die west staunen) as es ist "Jisrul Kremer"), geehrt Jisrul
Kremer bin ich in die Luft gespringen, ch'well sehen mit maine eigene Ojgen dem Kremer,
vin welchen ch'hob schojn a soj viel Artikel in verschiedene Zaiting gesehen indoch
persenlich nich gekennt. Nur wie is er, wie nemmt men den Kremer?Ch'hob gefiebert
far Najgierde in jugati umuzussi taamen, as me siecht gesindet men. Innem Feldzelt
vin'm Feldwebel is Kremer gesessen in Noticringen in sain Notizbichel gemacht, weist
wus dus is gewen? Ot der jinger Mann wus hotgebritet Rache of Kischnew, mir hoben
sich bald bekennt in z'is ins beide a Hochgenuß gewen, ch'hob mich glicklich gefihlt a sa*

Bensik z'hubn. R'hot mich gefregt, was fir Perschojn di bist, ich hob ihm alles erklärt mit hobben wichtiges diskutiert, azint zim Iker: Z'sammen sennen mir jenem Donnerschtig zim Schitzengraben arinter in gekämpft hobben mir einer neben andern, kein Wort hot Kremer wehrend dem Kampf verloren, erscht bei a Pause felgt er sich ze mir ausdrein in a Schmies angeknippt. Dem letzen Tug hot s'fajer 12 Schu ununterbrochen angehalten. Mit einmul hiest es "forwärts", der Feind hot sich z'rick gezogen, ich hob mich schnell zi Kremer imgedreiht in bam Arbel mit a G'dille a Zich getin: „Mir geihen vor", ober a zure, Kremer gibt sich kein Rihr, mit der Bichs in der Hand hot er gekniet wie frieher, mit sein ernsten, tiefen Blick, nur an die obigen Naseknochen s'inter der Stern is gewen a rund Kneppel arain gestezt in a kalchiger rojter Fleck arim wie a Buk vin a lang gtrugenem Zwicker, s'Harz hot sich in mir a Worf getin, oj Kremer is tojt! In vorwärts hot es gemißt geihn, in in main Kopp is nur gewen die eine Machschuwe: „Rache für Kischinew, N'kume far dem tajren Kremer", jo Ich leb ober Kremer ist tojt, s'ist schojn nuch dem Kampf, me kenn rasten, ich hob main Frajnd nicht mehr, ch'bin verjussimt ch'miß mich far dir vin'm Harz ubreden, obwohl ch'weiß s'wet Dich auch gitt krenken. Der Oberleitnant hot mit Tränen gegossen, er hot ihm gesollt dus Eiserne Kreiz auf der Brist heften.

Host noch allz vin meine Liebe Eltern nicht geehrt? Schraib mir oft, bist mich m'chaje! As haschem jisburach wet mir schenken s'Leben mit Gesind well Dir imjirzeh haschem die zweite Woche widder eppes schraiben, dus Beigele Papier is s'letzte wus ch'hob in Turnister gehat.

Bleib gesind in stark.

Jedidcho ojhawcho

Chajim.

"Revenge for Kishinev".

Translation of "Revenge for Kishinev."

God be praised. In camp, the 4th Marcheshvan ("eighth month", the second month of the civil year, the eighth month of the ecclesiastical year. Oct/Nov.) that is, the year 5675 after the creation of the world.

Dearest friend of my heart!

Yes, brother, I have risen from the dead. I lay in a dark, damp grave for 6 days. It's called a trench, and I am back amongst the living and have been transformed; but don't think that I am making jokes; this is not the time for that.

Last Thursday, I went to the trenches and bayonetted and fired, fired and bayonetted again, rested a little and then, go! I was lucky, I had a small flask of cognac that you sent me some weeks ago. I was able to use it to wet my whistle and do my duty with new courage.

Yes, good brother, I am alive, my Unsane Tokef has turned all to the good, once again, but my heart is still torn into pieces because of an emotional story; it will be particularly emotional for you: there was an attack two weeks ago and there was a dark-haired soldier beside me, he looked Hungarian, who I noticed because he continuously made notes in a small notebook during each lull in the fighting. There was no time to become acquainted because we were ordered to charge. I have already written to you about what that all looked like. I gritted my teeth and my neighbour growled: "Revenge for Kishinev", and the noble, gentle face turned into a beast-like grimace.

The attack lasted some 5 hours, and we drove the enemy from an important position. We rested all night on the battlefield. In the morning, I was so surprised and astonished; a Jewish corporal had saved the senior lieutenant from certain death during a night attack – the senior lieutenant's life was hanging by a thread; two Cossacks had attacked him with their sabers, and the Jewish corporal had saved him with two skilled strikes at the Cossacks. – I then tried to find out the name of the corporal (you will be astonished), and it is "Jisrul Kremer". I jumped into the air when I heard Jisrul Kremer, and I wanted to see Kremer with my own eyes. I have seen so many articles in various newspapers but never got to know him personally. But where was Kremer? I was feverish with curiosity and made great efforts, and what one seeks one finds. Kremer was sitting in a tent with a sergeant, making notes in his notebook, and do you know what? It was the young man who had said "Revenge for Kishinev".

We soon got to know one another, and it was a great joy for us both. I felt so happy to have a companion. He asked me what kind of a fellow you were, and I told him everything, we discussed important things.

Back to the main point: on the Thursday, we went to the trenches together and we fought side by side. Kremer didn't say a word during the fighting. Only during a break did he come and sit with me and light a cigarette. On the last day, the fighting continued for almost 12 hours without cease. Suddenly we heard the call; "Forwards", the enemy is pulling back. I quickly turned to Kremer and tugged his arm: "We're advancing." But oh, such pain. Kremer doesn't move. He was kneeling as before with his notebook in his hand, with his serious, deep face. Just above his nose was a round lump with a chalky red spot, and then it was like the temple of a long pince-nez. My heart turned over inside me. O, the pain of it, Kremer is dead! I had to go on the advance, and in my head there was only one thought: "Revenge for Kishinev; revenge for dead Kremer."

Yes, I am alive, but Kremer is dead. Now the battle is already over and we are able to rest. I no longer have my friend, I am an orphan.

For your sake, I have to persuade my heart to write to you, although I know it will upset you, too, very much. The senior lieutenant had tears streaming down his face. He was to have pinned the Iron Cross to Kremer's chest.

Do you still hear about everything from my dear parents?

Write to me often, you make me happy!

If the dear Lord wishes to let me live and be well, I will, God willing, write something to you again next week. This piece of paper is the last that I had in my backpack.

Stay healthy and strong,

Your loving friend,

Chajim.

Seder during wartime.

From a letter from senior NCO in the ... Reserve Infantry Regiment, Felix Rosenblüth, Berlin. E. near St. Q., 2nd of April 1915.

... We marched off from Mauchy-Lagache at 8.30 in the evening, the whole battalion in a marching column, the band ahead, and the weapons wagons and food wagons at the rear. Amongst these wagons was the mule team that our company had requisitioned so that it could increase the number of its wagons. You were celebrating Passover at home, the first evening of Seder. It was difficult to think about it even on the march, because the atmosphere amongst the men was too lively and humorous. When the major greeted us with the Punch and Judy question: "Are you all there?", and a thunderous "Yes" resounded towards him, all bonds to pious reserve were broken. Lamps were lit, a hellish noise was made on terrible self-made instruments, and so the nocturnal march with a glorious full moon resembled a torchlit polonaise. When we arrived in E. at midnight, I celebrated Passover after all, alone, admittedly, and only in a meagre way but as well as I could. My quarters were the opposite of the previous ones: a stuffy hole without windows or stove, with light coming from a second room which was filled with a noisy platoon and only embellished with a good, clean bed. When they were all snoring next door and R. had made his night camp in my little room, I took out the wine and the matzo, lit the candles and read the Haggadah. That was my first Seder evening, too little to mean anything by itself, but enough by which to remember earlier times.

Next day it was Passover and a genuine war-filled Passover celebration began. When I entered the office next morning, men jumped at me immediately with orders from the corps, regiment and battalion. Some orders were rescinded during the course of the day, but the wonderful finale was, at any rate, that by 3.30, cyclists were hurtling in from all sides with a regimental order: "All Jewish officers, NCOs and men are granted leave immediately to visit the Jewish service of worship at St. Q.; depart from the church at 4.10. Leave can be granted until tomorrow." You can imagine how happy I was! At 4.30, a staff baggage wagon full of Jewish soldiers (I was on the coachman's seat with R.) drove off towards St. Q. The 2nd Battalion had put another wagon at our disposal so that we didn't have to walk during Passover, and we accepted gratefully – the war knows no commandments. Even Rabbi Levy appeared with his car in the afternoon to procure our leave in St. Q.! He referred to a basic law of the Talmud, and I could only obediently agree with his behaviour.

St. Q. was a proper town with 54,000 inhabitants, physically unscathed by the war and with its urban features completely preserved; there were two taverns, the "Hamburger Hof" and the "Frankfurter Hof" – and ration cards for bread! A wonderful town with a glorious, unpretentious, gothic cathedral, very beautiful squares and the Champs Elysée, which would be impressive wherever they were. R. and I were assigned lovely quarters with a Monsieur Moguet, Rue de Cambrai 17, next to the commander's office; two magnificent rooms. We quickly took off our things and then went into the synagogue, a little prayer house, smaller but otherwise similar to our synagogue ... Altogether, there were 80 soldiers present. The French Jews seem to have been avoiding the synagogue since the occupation started. Only four of them

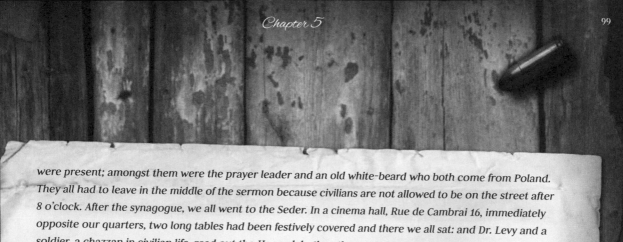

were present; amongst them were the prayer leader and an old white-beard who both come from Poland. They all had to leave in the middle of the sermon because civilians are not allowed to be on the street after 8 o'clock. After the synagogue, we all went to the Seder. In a cinema hall, Rue de Cambrai 16, immediately opposite our quarters, two long tables had been festively covered and there we all sat: and Dr. Levy and a soldier, a chazzan in civilian life, read out the Haggadah; then there was an abundance of good food to eat. I think they were all happy that they were celebrating their Judaism in war time and were able to come together as Jews; although I must confess that I felt very strongly: the Seder is a family celebration. Dr. Levy directed his words towards two Jewish nurses who were sitting to the side of him and praised them for their services to the Seder. Someone else spoke about Dr. Levy. The chazzan spoke smugly and showed himself to be, therefore ... tout comme chez nous ... (just as it is at home). Also, the fact that the French chazzan was insulted because he had been excluded during the days of celebration, pleased me as proof of the unity of Judaism: which chazzan in Israel would voluntarily step aside?!! But they were all grateful that they had been able to celebrate Passover in a dignified manner.

The next day, the 31st March, we went to the synagogue again, and I was called up to the Torah, which would please father. I was given shelishi. And then I swung myself into the car of an airman who happened to be going my way, and I was very quickly back in E. ...

Tonight, we will be marching again, through St. Q. as far as O., where we will take up quarters again. What is going to happen to us in the future, no one knows.

I send you all my love.
Your,
Felix.

AN DIE DEUTSCHEN MÜTTER!

Christliche und jüdische Helden haben gemei

12000 Juder

Blindwütiger Parteihass macht vo

Deutsche

duldet nicht, dass die jüdische Mu

Reichs

72 000
...ische Soldaten
...r das Vaterland
...Felde der Ehre
...allen

...ämpft und ruhen gemeinsam in fremder Erde.

...len im Kampf !

...Gräbern der Toten nicht Halt.

...auen,

...ihrem Schmerz verhohnt wird

...üdischer Frontsoldaten E.V.

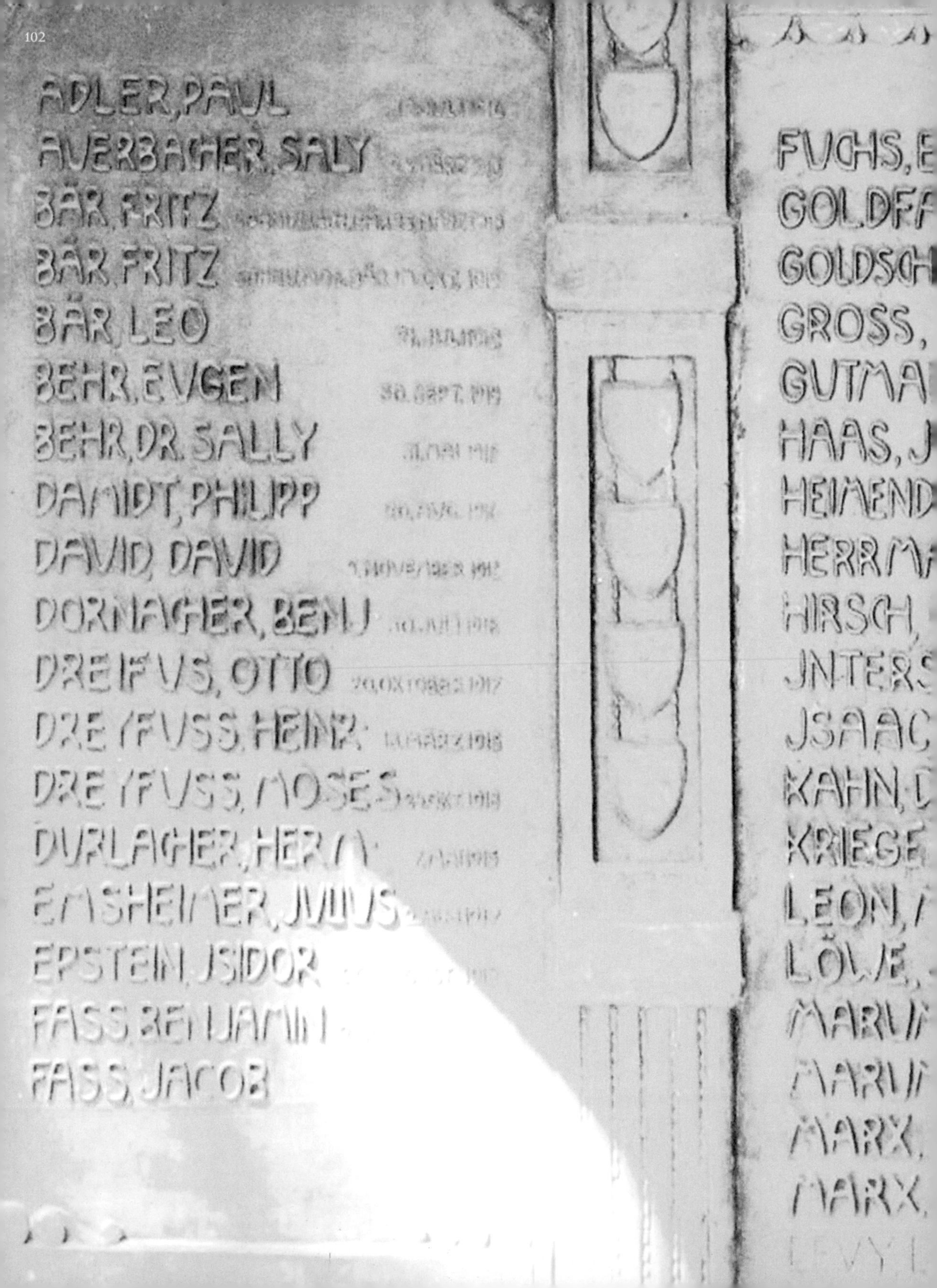

ADLER, PAUL

AVERBACHER, SALLY

BÄR, FRITZ

BÄR, FRITZ

BÄR, LEO

BEHR, EUGEN

BEHR, DR. SALLY

DAMDT, PHILIPP

DAVID, DAVID

DORNACHER, BENJ

DREIFUS, OTTO

DREYFUSS, HEINZ

DREYFUSS, MOSES

DURLACHER, HERM

EMSHEIMER, JULIUS

EPSTEIN, ISIDOR

FASS, BENJAMIN

FASS, JACOB

FUCHS,

GOLDFA

GOLDSCH

GROSS,

GUTMA

HAAS, J

HEIMEND

HERRM

HIRSCH,

JNTERS

JSAAC

KAHN, D

KRIEGE

LEON,

LÖWE,

MARUM

MARUM

MARX,

MARX

LEVY

MAYER, RICHARD
MUNK, MORITZ
ODENHEIMER, JULIUS
PALM, HERMANN
PORITZKY, ISIDOR
RICHEIMER, LUDWIG
ROSENBERGER, MICH.
ROSENFELDER, MAX
ROSENHEIM, ULRICH
ROTHEIMER, SIMON
SCHWARZWÄLDER, GUST.
STRAUSS, HEINRICH
TRAUB, MAX
WEIL, LEO
WESTHEIMER, HUGO
WILDBERG, ADOLF
WIMPFHEIMER, ARTUR
WOLF, WILLI

A short glossary of Jewish words and phrases

Avinu Malkeinu
"Our Father, Our King", a prayer recited during religious service on Rosh Hashanah and Yom Kippur and on the Ten Days of Repentance, which last from Rosh Hashanah through to Yom Kippur.

Awelim
A mourner.

Baal Milchomo
Soldier.

Bar Kokhba revolt
This took place from 132 – 136 C.E. It was the last of the Jewish-Roman Wars. and the third major Jewish rebellion in the Province of Judea against the Roman Empire. The Jewish commander, Simon bar Kokhba, ("son of the star" – his real name was Simon ben Kosiba) was acclaimed as a Messiah who could resurrect Israel. For two years, an independent state of Israel in parts of Judea was maintained until six Roman legions and other sections of the Roman Army, finally ended the revolt. Kochbaner are followers of Simon Kochba. "Rasse" is a German word meaning "race" or "nation". "Bar-kochbanerrasse", therefore, would be a race of people following the spirit of Simon bar Kochba.

Barkochbahain
A "Hain" in German is a copse or a grove.

Baruch HaShem
Blessed be the name or blessed be God.

Beis HaChaim
A Jewish cemetery, also beit kvarot.

Bekowet
Honourable, cosy.

Bentshing/bentshen
To bless a person or say a blessing.

Berches - or challah
Bread from southern Germany. Berches was the name used in the Middle Ages, adopted by the Jews for the Sabbath.

Beth HaMidrash
House of learning, or study.

Besamim
A spice box with elaborate ornamentation to honour the Mitzvah of Havdalah.

Birkhat Ha-Gomeyl
A blessing given after danger has passed.

Bracha
A blessing before eating. (brachot pl.)

Challah
Bread from southern Germany. Berches was the name used in the Middle Ages, adopted by the Jews for the Sabbath.

Chamisha Asar Bishvat
The 15th of the month of Shevat. A Jewish holiday celebrating the New Year of the Trees, (trees begin to blossom) one of four New Year celebrations.

Chazzan
Someone who leads the congregation in prayer. Most Jews will perform this role on occasion.

Cheder
An elementary school teaching the basics of Judaism. Widespread in Europe prior to end of the 18th century. Lessons were held in the house of the teacher paid for by the Jewish community or parents. It was usual for boys only to attend classes, girls were taught at home by their mothers.

Chol Hamoed
The intermediate days of Passover and Succoth which come in between the beginning and final holy days of both celebrations.

Cum grano salis
With a grain of salt.

Dayan
A judge in a Jewish religious court.

Daven
To pray, Yiddish; derives from the same Latin root as the English, "divine".

Eretz Ysrael
The Land of Israel, roughly the area of Palestine, Canaan, the Promised Land and the Holy Land. In Genesis, God promised the land to Abraham's descendants through Isaac his son and to the descendants of Abraham's grandson Jacob, the Israelites.

Gemoro
The element of the Talmud consisting of rabbinical analysis and commentary on the Mishnah.

Haggadah
"Telling"; a text that sets out the order of the Seder at Passover. It is a commandment to read the Haggadah at the Seder table. The commandment is to "tell your son" about the liberation of the Jews from slavery in Egypt as described in the Torah. (Book of Exodus.)

HaKodosh Baruch Hu
The Holy One, may He be praised.

Hanukkah
(Chanukah) an eight-day holiday commemorating the rededication of the Holy Temple in Jerusalem in the 2nd century BC during the Maccabean Revolt. The lights on the nine-branched Hanukkah candelabra are lit, one more each night.

HaShem Yisborach
May His name be blessed.

Havdalah
A ritual required during Motzei Shabbat (the hours after the end of Shabbat). The word Havdalah means, "separation". Listening to the Havdalah blessings determines the end of Shabbat. Shabbat must be declared to be at an end if anyone wants to lights the Havdalah candle or perform any prohibited activity.

Hedad
A shout, cheer.

Hoshana Rabbah
The seventh and last day of the Jewish holiday of Succoth, the "Festival of Booths".

Judah
The Kingdom of Judah was a Jewish state sited in the southern Levant. It is also known as the Southern Kingdom to differentiate it from the Kingdom of Israel, and probably arose around the BCE.

Kashrut Kosher
Kashrut are the laws governing Jewish food. One of the laws forbids cooking or eating meat and milk together. An observant Jew will wait for up to six hours after eating meat or poultry before eating dairy products.

Kesiwo wachasimo toiwo
Best wishes for the New Year. (L'shanah tovah tikatev v'taihatem - may you be inscribed and sealed (in the book of life) for a good year. Also, Ketivah tovah - may you be inscribed.)

Kiddush
A blessing recited over grape juice or wine before a meal, to sanctify Shabbat and Jewish holidays; "Blessed are You, O Lord our God, Ruler of the universe, creator of the fruit of the vine."

Kittel
A white robe, the burial shroud for male Jews. Ashkenazi Jews wear it, also, on special occasions. Known as Sargenes in Western Europe. Worn by married men on Yom Kippur and occasionally on Rosh Hashanah.

Kol Nidre
A prayer recited in the synagogue at the beginning of evening service on the Day of Atonement. Opposed by rabbinic authorities and expunged from prayer books by many Western European communities.

Lewaja
The funeral.

Lekovid
Honoured, to honour.

Luach
A Jewish calendar.

Maariv
The Tefillah recited each night. Maariv commemorates the burning of sacrificial remains in the Temple each night. The ritual was conceived by the patriarch Jacob. He spent the night in contemplation of God, teaching his descendants to do the same.

Maccabees
A rebel army that fought against the Greeks, leading to the Hanukkah victory over them, 200 CE. They took control of Judea. Judah Maccabee was the son of the Jewish priest Mattathias.

Machzor/Mahzor
The prayer book used on Rosh Hashanah and Yom Kippur. (Pl. Machsorim.)

Ma'oz Tzur
The beginning of the Hanukkah song, Stronghold of Rock. (God)

Maskir Neschomaus
A memorial for the dead.

Matzo or Matzah
(Pl. Matzos/Matzot). An unleavened bread eaten during the week-long holiday of Passover.

Mazel
Luck or fortune.

Menucha
Peaceful, rest.

Mezuman
A prepared gathering. 3 men eating bread as part of a meal must form a mezuman and invite the others to pray. The invitation is called a zimmun. Mezuman bentshen = praying together at the table.

Mi chamocha
Who is like you?

Mikveh
A bath used in Judaism for ritual immersion. The word means, "collection".

Mincha
The afternoon prayers. In the Temple in Jerusalem, meal offerings, from which the name "Mincha" derives, were made to accompany sacrifices.

Minyan
A quorum of ten or more Jewish males over 13 years of age, which is required before a religious service can be held.

Misrach
The east, the Holy Land.

Mitzvah
God's precepts and commandments.

Motzei Shabbos Kodesh
This is the time in the evening when three stars appear in the sky, and the end of the Sabbath.

Musaf
"Additional" prayers that are recited by conservative and orthodox congregations on Shabbat and major Jewish holidays such as Chol HaMoed or Rosh Chodesh.

Neilah
The closing service of Yom Kippur. Neilah means "closing", referring to the symbolic closing of the gates of Heaven.

Neworech Elaukenu
"Let us exalt his name together".

Oren
Say prayers, pray.

Passover

Commemorates the Exodus, the flight of the ancient Israelites, when they were freed from Egyptian slavery. It begins on the 15th day of the month of Nisan, (March or April), and continues for seven or eight days.

Rabbi

One who teaches the Torah, from the Hebrew "My Master."

Rosh Chodesh

The first day of every month in the Hebrew calendar, indicated by a new moon.

Rosh Hashanah

New Year.

Sefer Torah

A parchment Torah scroll on which the five books of Moses are written by hand in Hebrew. It is kept in the Ark in the synagogue and sections of it are read publicly on Shabbat, Jewish holidays, fast days, and Monday and Thursday mornings. A minyan is required for public readings.

Seforim

Books, Torah rolls.

Selichot

Atonement prayers.

Shabbat Chol Ha-mo'ed Sukkot

The Sabbath during Chol Ha-mo'ed on the days between Passover and Succoth. Torah readings are augmented by Ecclesiastes being read aloud in the synagogue in its entirety. Sukkot/Succoth is the Feast of Booths. It was celebrated in the month of Tishrei (late September to late October) on the 15th day. It was a commandment for Hebrews to make a pilgrimage to the temple in Jerusalem. The holiday lasts seven days, eight in the diaspora. Succoth reminds the Jews of the small huts in which the Israelites lived during the 40 years in the desert following the Exodus.

Sabbath Shirah

The Sabbath of song. The Shirat hayam is the song of praise to God for leading the Israelites from Egypt through the Sea of Reeds.

Seder

The two first evenings of the Passover celebrations. The story of the Exodus from Egypt is related within families.

Shalom aleichem

Peace be upon you, a traditional form of greeting amongst Jews worldwide.

Shacharit

The daily morning prayer.

Shas

The Mishnah or Mishna is the first important redaction of oral Jewish traditions known as the Oral Torah. Mostly written in Hebrew, whereas the Talmud is written in Judeao-Aramaic.

Shelishi

Third. The aliyah (pl. aliyot) is a Torah reading. The aliyot for the Shabbat are: (1) Kohen (2) Levi (3) Shelishi (4) Revi'i (5) Hamishi (6) Shishi (7) Shevi'i (8) Maftir.

Shemini Atzeret

The eighth day of assembly during the Festival of Succoth, celebrated in the Hebrew month of Tishrei on the 22nd day.

Shir Hama'alot
The song of ascents.

Shofar
A horn, usually made from a ram's horn. In ancient Israel it announced Rosh Chodesh, the New Moon and called people together. Also blown on Rosh Hashanah to mark the beginning of the New Year.

Shul
A Yiddish word for synagogue.

Siddur
Prayer book. (Pl. Siddurim.)

Simcha shel Mitzvah
Happiness in fulfilling a Mitzvah.

Simchat Torah
The cycle of annual public Torah reading comes to an end with this celebration, "Rejoicing with the Torah."

Simcha
Is happiness, or joy. An important concept in Jewish philosophy. Someone who is happy is better able to serve God and perform daily activities than someone depressed or unhappy.

Talmud
(Traditional: Shas) has two parts, the Mishnah and Gemora/Gemoro, and is a central text of mainstream Judaism. It is a record of rabbinic discussions relating to Jewish history, law, philosophy, ethics etc.

Tashlikh
In Hebrew means "casting off", a ritual during the afternoon of Rosh Hashanah. The sins of the past year are symbolically cast off by throwing pieces of bread or other food into a large quantity of flowing water, a lake or the sea, etc. Tashlikh stems from the Middle Ages, inspired by a verse spoken by the prophet Micah: God will cast all our sins into the depths of the sea. (Micah 7:19.)

Tefillah
Prayer, prayer book.

Tefillin
A set of small black leather boxes are strapped around the upper arm. They contain scrolls of parchment on which are hand-written verses from the Torah. Observant Jews wear them every weekday morning. The head tefillin is placed above the forehead.

Trefo
Forbidden foods.

Triple Entente
The alliance between Britain, France and Russia formed by the signing of the 1907 Anglo-Russian Entente. The Triple Alliance was formed by Germany, Austro-Hungary and Italy.

Tzitzit
Ritual fringes with special knots, which are attached to the four corners of the prayer shawl.

Unsane Tokef
A prayer, cantorial, recited as an introduction to the Kedushah prayer. "Let us now declare the might of this day's holiness, for it is awesome and fearsome."

Ve Tiheru et Mikdasheikha Ve hedliku Nerot Lehodot veLehalel LeShimkha HaGado

A prayer recited during Hanukkah, thanking God for saving the Jewish people. "... purified Your Temple and lit candles to thank and praise Your great name."

Yehi Ratzon

May it be Your will.

Yehudi

A Jew.

Yeshiva

A Talmud high school, for Torah and Talmud study. Hebrew, "sitting".

Yiddish

It is an amalgam of languages consisting mainly of High German with Hebrew, Slavic and some Romance languages and is spoken by Jews throughout the world. It originated in the Rhineland in Germany in about the 10th century AD with the Ashkenazi Jews, spreading across to Eastern Europe and thence to other countries around the world. Famous Ashkenazi Jews: Sigmund Freud; Gustav Mahler; Golda Meir; George Gershwin; Anne Frank; Heinrich Heine; Albert Einstein.

Yirah

Awe, devotion.

Yom Kippur

The Day of Atonement, the holiest and most solemn Jewish festival.

Yom tov

"Good day" but refers also to holidays. Jewish holidays are considered as holy or secular commemorations of important events in the past. There are similar duties and prohibitions as on the Sabbath, except that it is permitted to cook, carry, and transfer fire from another flame.

Zedoch tazil mimowes

German Yiddish. Good deeds will save one from death.

Zemirot

To sing or make music. The majority of Sabbath zemirot songs originated in Spain when Hebrew poetry was influenced by Arabic poetry. They praise God and the Sabbath.

Other terms.

Blue beans
Lead, bullets.

Franctireur
French sharpshooters, snipers.

Landwehr/Wehrmann/Landsturm
The Landwehr was a branch of the German Army. In status it came third after the regular army and the reserves. Generally older soldiers formed the ranks of the Landwehr divisions, having passed from the reserves. Their role was seen initially as one of occupation and security.

Scharpie/Charpie
Lint, used for protecting wounds. Plucked from cotton or linen and replaced later by cotton wool.

Tannenberg
A battle between the Germans and the Russians in East Prussia in August 1914, which actually took place in Allenstein 30 km away. It resulted in the almost complete destruction of the Russian 2nd Army and virtually ended the Russian invasion of East Prussia. The name was given to the battle to counter the defeat of the Teutonic Knights in 1410 at Tannenberg by the Poles, Lithuanians and Tartars.

Uhlans
Polish light cavalry armed with pistols, sabres and lances.

Wolffsohn, David
9th October 1856 – 15th September 1914. A Jewish Lithuanian businessman and early Zionist, he was the second president of the Zionist Organisation.